SHELLEY UNBOUND

Discovering Frankenstein's True Creator

BY SCOTT DOUGLAS de HART

SHELLEY UNBOUND

Discovering Frankenstein's True Creator

BY SCOTT DOUGLAS de HART

FERAL HOUSE

FOREWORD

BY JOSEPH P. FARRELL

When my good friend of almost twenty years, Dr. Scott D. de Hart, and I were working on our previous book, *Transhumanism: A Grimoire of Alchemical Altars and Agendas for the Transformation of Man*, we very quickly recognized the crucial role that literature had played in disseminating the memes of the alchemical transformation of human consciousness, culture, and society. We zeroed in on Oscar Wilde, Dante Alighieri, and most importantly, Percy Bysshe Shelley as the alchemical authors par excellence, but it soon became clear that, of all these, it was Shelley who was the most crucial, and most complex.

Dr. de Hart quickly uncovered so much material that threw the whole academic farrago of Mary Shelley's authorship of that most alchemical of novels, *Frankenstein*, into a cocked hat, that over the course of several conversations we became convinced that the topic of its authorship, and the alchemical and even Illuminist themes within it, deserved a full treatment of its own—and that Scott should be the one to outline the burgeoning, and largely ignored, case against Mary Shelley's and for Percy Shelley's authorship of the famous novel, and more importantly to show how deeply steeped it is in the themes and memes of alchemical, esoteric, and Illuminati lore.

So it behooves us to state the case in a high overview and as succinctly as possible: Percy Bysshe Shelley placed the setting of *Frankenstein* squarely in the middle of a vast conspiracy; he set it in Ingolstadt,[i] Bavaria, home and headquarters to the celebrated Bavarian Illuminati of Ingolstadt University Professor of Canon Law, Adam Weishaupt.

Shelley, as Dr. de Hart will detail in these pages, was enamored of the idea of a perfection of mankind, a possibility he saw would emerge once man was free of the intellectual constraints of Christianity, and able to develop the full potentials of science and all that it entailed for human life and society—and in this, the "perfectabilism" of Illuminism offered Shelley a manifesto in which to couch his novel.

Adam Weishaupt (1748–1830) was the conspirator's conspirator, the founder of the notorious Bavarian Illuminati. As Dr. de Hart will detail in the main text, Percy Shelley was more than familiar with the machinations of this secret society, having read Abbé Barruel's history of Jacobinism during the French Revolution, in which the Illuminati played a prominent role—in Barruel's opinion—in unleashing the forces that would eventually overturn the French monarchy.

Another contemporary of Abbé Barruel, John Robison, wrote in his 1798 exposé of the Illuminati,[i] *Proofs of a Conspiracy*, that at its height, the order had initiated into its ranks all but two professors of the entire University of Ingolstadt. Given his thorough knowledge of matters pertaining to the Illuminati, we may reasonably assume that Percy Bysshe Shelley, in choosing to set *Frankenstein* at the notorious headquarters of the Illuminati, was more than familiar with the vast influence of the Order there.

But why would the Order appeal to Shelley in the first place?

As Dr. de Hart ably demonstrates in this book, the Order's views were not only similar in their revolutionary cultural goals—to weaken and eventually marginalize the influence of Christianity within Western culture—to Percy Shelley's, but they were in the final analysis identical. Weishaupt, who had adopted the code name Spartacus for himself, after the famous leader of the slaves' rebellion in ancient Rome, wrote to fellow Illuminatus Baron Knigge in 1778:

> ...in particular, every person shall be made a spy on another and on all around him. Nothing can escape our sight; by these means we shall readily discover who are contented, and receive with relish the peculiar state-doctrines and religious opinions that are laid before them; and, at last, the trust-worthy alone will be admitted to a participation of the whole maxims and political constitutions of the Order. In a council composed of such members we shall labour at the contrivance of means to drive by degrees the enemies of reason and of humanity out of the world, and to establish a peculiar morality and religion fitted for the great Society of mankind.[ii]

The "enemies of reason" were, of course, clerics and ministers of Christianity.

Elsewhere, Weishaupt would reveal even more of his attitude and agenda to fellow Illuminatus Baron Knigge, when expounding on a particular degree of initiation into the Order:

> One would almost imagine, that this degree, as I have managed it, is genuine Christianity, and that its end was to free the Jews from slavery. I say, that Free Masonry is concealed Christianity. My explanation of the hieroglyphics, at least, proceeds on this supposition; and as I explain things, no man need be ashamed of being a Christian. Indeed I afterwards throw away this name, and substitute Reason. But I assure you this is no small affair; a new religion, and a new state-government...You may think that this is my chief work...[iii]

The social and cultural program of the Illuminati, in other words, was a total one.

As Dr. de Hart demonstrates in these pages, these were goals that Percy Shelley most definitely shared, choosing to realize them through the beguiling beauty of his poems and the themes touched upon in them, and more importantly, in *Frankenstein*. In turning to literature to realize his alchemical and revolutionary goals, Shelley was again echoing a preoccupation of Weishaupt's Illuminati.

Again, Weishaupt anticipates yet another alchemical man of letters, Oscar Wilde, when he wrote "Nothing would be more profitable to us than a right history of mankind,"[iv] an insight that Wilde would epitomize in his essay "The Critic as Artist" in the words "the one duty we owe to history is to re-write it." Shelley, as Dr. de Hart shows, beat Wilde to the punch, and realized the alchemical nature of literature first. In this, too, he was well steeped in the Illuminist agenda and methods, for yet again, Weishaupt would write that in order to aid in the agenda of the transformation of Western culture and society,

> We must acquire the direction of education—of church management—of the professorial chair, and of the pulpit. We must bring our opinions into fashion by every art—spread them among the people by the help of young writers. We must preach the warmest concern for humanity, and make people indifferent to all other relations. We must take care that our writers be well puffed, and that the Reviewers do not depreciate them; therefore we must endeavour by every means to gain over the Reviewers and Journalists; and we must also try to gain the booksellers, who in time will see that it is their interest to side with us.[v]

Weishaupt could not have hoped for a more brilliant and gifted young writer than Percy Bysshe Shelley, for though there is no evidence that Shelley was ever a formal member of the Order, he had, through his own reading of Abbé Barruel and his own esoteric studies—a preoccupation Dr. de Hart skillfully demonstrates in the main text—imbibed the alchemical agenda of Illuminism.

Indeed, as you will learn in these pages, Shelley was a prophet, anticipating the transhumanist thinkers of the late twentieth and early twenty-first centuries that Dr. de Hart and I reviewed in our previous book, *Transhumanism: A Grimoire of Alchemical Altars and the Agenda for the Transformation of Man,* by almost two hundred years, pouring his visions forth in poems of incomparable beauty and genius, and epitomizing it all in that transhumanist alchemical masterpiece *Frankenstein*—and you could not have a better guide through this dark and magical forest than Dr. de Hart. His case for Percy Shelley's authorship of the novel is solid, and in the final analysis, almost irrefutable. It certainly will not gladden the entrenched interests of modern academic literary criticism, but it is a case that needs to be made, for so long as the novel's true author remains unknown, its dark yet brilliant themes, its alchemical, transhumanist purpose, will be—as they have been—profoundly misunderstood. This is a valuable, and in my opinion, indispensible contribution not only to literary criticism, but more importantly to our understanding of the modern transhumanist world emerging all around us. Shelley was its prophet, and Dr. de Hart is, as you will now see, the capable expositor of Shelley's vision.

—JOSEPH P. FARRELL, D.PHIL. (OXON) 2012

i John Robison, A.M., *Proofs of a Conspiracy* (Western Islands, 1967), p. 77.
ii Ibid., p. 77.
iii Robison, *Proofs of a Conspiracy*, p. 85.
iv Ibid., p. 91.
v Robison, *Proofs of a Conspiracy*, p. 109.

DEDICATION

~

To Wesley Randall, Calvin Thomas, Alexander Avery,
and Bennett Douglas Butera de Hart, my sons.

~

To Gary and Jacqueline, my parents.

~

To Joseph P. Farrell, my friend, colleague, and
scholar of scholars.

~

And
To the Angel who must forever believe in Plato's soul mate.
You made a believer out of me.

"A ray of electric-black alchemy Swept thru my soul today. The means to heal. All is one."

—S.D. DE HART

TABLE OF CONTENTS

INTRODUCTION

Percy Unbound

The World was to me a secret, which I desired to discover.
— Victor Frankenstein, *Frankenstein (1818)*
Anonymous [1]

On the 8th of July, 1822, less than a month before his thirtieth birthday, Percy Bysshe Shelley drowned at sea. Nearly two hundred years later, Shelley was graciously given partial credit for assisting his then-mistress and later to be wife, Mary, on her first novel, *Frankenstein, or The Modern Prometheus.* The extent of his contribution is generally relegated to serving as an editor and a sort of literary agent. He was, after all, a published poet, a friend of England's infamous poet Lord George Gordon Byron, and an acquaintance of the ailing young poet John Keats. Who better than Mary's well-connected accomplished partner in life, Percy, to advise, edit, and encourage her in writing the tale of the manmade creature seeking vengeance on its Creator?

Charles Robinson, professor of English at the University of Delaware and highly regarded *Frankenstein* authority, writes

We may conclude that he [Percy] contributed at least 4,000 to 5,000 words to this 72,000-word count novel. Despite the number of Percy's words, the novel was conceived and mainly written by Mary Shelley, as attested not only by others in their circle (e.g. Byron, Godwin, Claire and Charles Clairmont, Leigh Hunt) but by the nature of the manuscript evidence in the surviving pages of the Draft. [2]

Despite Mr. Robinson's credentials and well documented research on *Frankenstein*, the evidence argues for a second look, one which on further consideration will suggest a far more hideous story of a creature, Shelley himself, whose life not only parallels that of Victor Frankenstein but equally that of the creature whose intelligence and unique nature were hardly fit for a long span in community with mankind. This is the story of another *Frankenstein*, Percy Bysshe Shelley, the anonymous author of the story by the same name.

FRANKENSTEIN UNBOUND

Conspiracy theories and their originators are generally considered reckless upstarts, unless the weight of evidence begins to lean heavily on the side of a "conspiracy"; at that point the theory is no longer a fringe idea but becomes necessary to consider. New evidence, or a careful reexamination of old evidence, may be used to clear convicted felons, and thereafter the "unlikely possibility" suddenly becomes the most likely alternative. This book is a study in facts; a book offering an alternative solution regarding the author of *Frankenstein* and this "theory" will rely upon a consideration of old evidence set forward in a new light.

I want to dispel the idea that this book is an attack on the person or integrity of Mary Shelley. It is not an anti-feminist polemic nor is it a shot across the bow at the many respected and well-intentioned Percy Bysshe Shelley, Mary Shelley, and *Frankenstein* scholars. It is my contention that there was an initial conspiracy by the author of *Frankenstein* to hide his identity—Percy Bysshe Shelley—which soon thereafter turned into a second-stage conspiracy to attribute the work to Mary and thereby keep the true author's identity from ever being known. In order to pull off this hoax it was absolutely necessary that Mary be a fully committed collaborator in the scheme. In this manner I ascribe the highest honor to Mary Shelley for accomplishing and maintaining the desire of her late husband: living a lie for the sake of his will and her love for him.

Let us be clear about one thing up front, *Frankenstein* is not a horror story. It is not merely a contest-winning tale born from a stormy summer in Geneva. *Frankenstein* was not conceived in a dream nor in the mind of a young woman who had run away from her father to join her life to a radical young poet. *Frankenstein*'s iconic status in the feminist canon of English literature has made the question of authorship as closed as that of Moses' authorship of the Bible's Pentateuch among evangelical Christians. Cursed are those who suggest a reexamination of the evidence, and damned are those who dare trample underfoot the sacrosanct agenda which has become more important than the historical evidence. Nonetheless, history is a far more astute judge of truth than those who create and protect agendas. *Frankenstein* is the work of human hands, its message is earthly, its authorship is fair game, and though the critics will gnash their teeth in the face of the following evidence, the time has come for *Frankenstein*'s anonymous author to be given credit for his tale. It is humanity's duty to inquire after truth and to assign credit where credit is due, for our goal is advancement rather than entrenched ignorance. *Frankenstein* is an autobiographical story of Percy Bysshe Shelley.

From the moment that *Frankenstein* was set loose upon the world in published form, critics began to raise questions over the authorship. An anonymous critic writing for *Knights Quarterly* in 1824 argues with great acumen that Percy Shelley must have authored the first edition of *Frankenstein*. The critic reasons by comparing Mary Shelley's 1823 romantic novel *Valperga* to *Frankenstein*:

> But whence arises the extreme inferiority of *Valperga*? I can account for it only by supposing that Shelley wrote the first [*Frankenstein*], though it was attributed to his wife, and that she really wrote the last [*Valperga*].[3]

Knights Quarterly is not the only nineteenth-century review to observe the poetic talent and genius of Percy Shelley in *Frankenstein*. The renowned historic novelist, playwright, and poet, Sir Walter Scott, identified the hand of Percy Shelley immediately and noted that the author of *Frankenstein* had "uncommon powers of poetic imagination."[4] In his attempt to remain unidentified as the author of *Frankenstein*, Percy Shelley insisted to Mr. Scott that he was not the author but only "superintended" the book through the press "during the Author's absence." Naturally, *if* Mary were the author, it stands as a boldfaced lie that the author was absent during the final stages of publishing. Additionally, the *Frankenstein Notebooks*, or the manuscripts of the novel, have clear proof that Percy Shelley, *if not* its author, was instrumental in more than superintending the book through the press. Even Dr. Charles Robinson credits Percy Shelley with enough hard evidence to prove his role as far greater than a superintendent. Finally, as an act of desperation, Mary Shelley wrote to Sir Walter Scott and insisted, "I am anxious to prevent your *continuing* in the mistake of supposing Mr. Shelley guilty of a juvenile attempt of mine ..."[v] It is apparent that the wool was not pulled over all discerning eyes when *Frankenstein* was first published.

This book will prove that such calculated subterfuge concerning authorship by Percy Shelley is in itself one of the surest signs of his hand in writing *Frankenstein*. Although anonymity at first glance appears to be a clever attempt to hide an author's identity, for Percy Shelley it was virtually his *very signature* and left an indelible literary fingerprint on *Frankenstein* which is as clear today as when he wrote the novel in 1818. This book will present evidence that Shelley's *modus operandi* was to hide beneath pseudonyms and to use anonymity in order to stir the public's imagination to contemplate thoughts which if taken up and acted upon would create a major revolution in politics, personal relationships, and religion. Additionally, he was well aware that the penalty for inciting such movements was imprisonment or death, a strong incentive to play his part from behind the curtain where the veil of secrecy might hide his multitude of sins.

Two books are worthy of mention at the start of this investigation: Phyllis Zimmerman's *Shelley's Fiction,* published in 1998 by Darami Press (Los Angeles, CA), and John Lauritsen's *The Man who Wrote Frankenstein*, published in 2007 by Pagan Press (Dorchester, MA). Both books take a critical approach to the authorship of *Frankenstein*, arrive at the conclusion that Percy Shelley was its author, and are important sources to be considered alongside of the present study. Zimmerman's research, acquaintance with poetic style, comprehensive awareness of Shelley's poetry and prose, and her astute literary analysis are an invaluable aid to any reader seeking to understand Percy Shelley. Equally worthy of recognition, Lauritsen sets forward a unique thesis concerning the underlying theme of homosexuality in *Frankenstein*. His argument is supported by an analysis of writing style and historical facts surrounding the writing of *Frankenstein*. While I am not in agreement with his nearly convincing homosexuality-focused thesis, I am appreciative of his analysis supporting Shelley's authorship and I am therefore indebted to his work as a groundbreaking new approach to the question of authorship.

This book will rely more heavily upon details that are not within the scope of Zimmerman's or Lauritsen's works, in particular the biographical overlapping of Percy Shelley's life, education, philosophy, and writings as they relate to the story of Victor Frankenstein and his creature. Special attention will be given to Shelley's lifelong attachment to the subjects of atheism, alchemy, Platonic love in human relationships, and the Bavarian Illuminati. To understand *Frankenstein* is to become familiar with its author, a rare genius whose life was every bit as eccentric as that of the creature's isolated maker; as lonely and conniving as the unique creature; and as dangerous as both creator and creature.

ACKNOWLEDGMENTS

To paraphrase the words of Mary Shelley, I do not owe a single suggestion for the ideas in this book to any other. I recognize that few would dare to attach their name to such a project tempting the ire of the English reading community and its scholars who have long and arduously defended the authorship of *Frankenstein* to Mary Shelley. While I do not wish to attribute any ideas or faults herein to any others, I am obligated to offer my appreciation for support to many, beginning with Adam Parfrey, my publisher at Feral House and Jessica Parfrey, whose communications and assistance were most helpful. I am especially indebted to Joseph P. Farrell, my friend, co-author of *Grid of the Gods* (Adventures Unlimited) and *Transhumanism: A Grimoire of Alchemical Agendas* (Feral House), and deep scholar who believed in and encouraged me in this project before any others knew of my ideas on *Frankenstein*. I am grateful to my enthusiastic and inquisitive students at Oak Hills High School who, in their General English course, have read with great interest the 1818 edition of *Frankenstein* and have been studious with their questions, written assignments, and continual inquiries as to my research relating to Percy Shelley's role in the writing of *Frankenstein*. To the OHHS Poets & Quill club, thank you for your enthusiasm to study the great Poets and keep their words alive today! To the faculty members who were privy to the research and could always be counted on for support (Kelly Roy, Stephanie Barden, Barbara Caballero, Jenny Bell and in particular Allison Rohr), thank you for your well-timed encouraging words, they were needed. I also owe my appreciation to my oldest friends, Mike deFusco and Scott Cantrell, who have encouraged my eccentricities, supported my research ideas, and encouraged me in all of my life projects; I thank you. I must also acknowledge my two sisters (Lisa and Lori) for their grace and commitment to the Spirit of Truth as they have encouraged me throughout the years. Additionally, to Nancy Kay Randall, heaven is surely your reward for enduring me and my endeavors for nearly twenty years. To the radiant Moon, the Emerald daughter who glows, and to Marlen who swims deeply, your love is inspirational. Laura, your presence in the final stages of editing opened new vistas for the author of this work, thank you is not sufficient.

Finally, I owe my *deepest* eternal gratitude to my children, Wesley, Calvin, Alexander, and Bennett, for sacrificing their father's *spare* time while this book was being written, you are my heart and soul, my very pride. To my loving parents, Gary and Jacque de Hart, thank you for the casita and for the gift that you instilled within me to see life through the eyes of an artist and to think as a philosopher continually asking questions rather than relying upon the time-accepted status quo opinions which had been conveniently prepackaged and handed down through the centuries, thank you will never be sufficient.

SCOTT D. DE HART, PH.D.
LOS ANGELES, CALIFORNIA 2012

1 Mary Shelley, *Frankenstein, or the Modern Prometheus*, D.L. Macdonald & Kathleen Scherf, eds., *The Original 1818 Text* (Broadview Press Ltd.: 1994), p. 61

2 Mary Shelley, *The Original Frankenstein, Two New Versions*, Charles Robinson, ed., (Random House: 2008), p. 25

3 Anonymous, *Knights Quarterly*, August 1824

4 Walter Scott, "Remarks on *Frankenstein, or The Modern Prometheus*; a Novel," *Blackwood's Edinburgh Magazine*, v. 2 no. 12 (March 1818), p. 619

5 Mary Shelley, *Letters of Mary Shelley*, ed. Bennett, 1:71

PERCY BYSSHE SHELLEY (4 AUGUST 1792 — 8 JULY 1822)

CHAPTER 1

THE PROBLEM WITH PREFACES

Whence, I often asked myself, did this principle of life proceed?

— Victor Frankenstein, *Frankenstein, or the Modern Prometheus,*
1818 1ˢᵗ Edition
Anonymous [1]

INITIAL OBSERVATIONS

Frankenstein: The name is synonymous with a slow-moving, half-witted, oversized monster that was created from a dead man's body and bestowed with a murderer's brain by an obsessed scientist. Hollywood has so framed the creature's identity in the public image that few today are aware that it was the *creator* and not the creature who is actually Frankenstein. Fewer still would raise an eyebrow that the scientist's name in the 1931 Universal horror movie was Henry Frankenstein, whereas the main character in the novel was in fact *Victor* Frankenstein. One wonders how many are aware that the combined parts for the framing and creation of the so-called *fiend* were both human and animal in this early transhumanistic experiment of Frankenstein.[2] It is curious that the public perception and confusion of identity regarding "Frankenstein" is a mirror image of the confusion over authorship that was embedded into the novel from the day of its initial publication in 1818. How few today are aware that *Frankenstein, or the Modern Prometheus* was first published anonymously? Fewer still are aware that the first critics ascribed credit to *Percy* Shelley rather than Mary Shelley as the author of the 1818 novel. Is it accidental, coincidental, or intentional that one of the most widely read novels in the English language is shrouded beneath a veil of confusion? It is the argument of this book that the facts demonstrate intention rather than coincidence, and misdirection rather than confusion. *Frankenstein* is a biography of Percy Shelley, or perhaps is better described as a fictionalized *auto*biography by the young Romantic poet who died in 1822, shortly before his thirtieth birthday.

Evidence within the novel suggests certain driving influences were at work upon the author of *Frankenstein*. Chief among the obvious influences revealed in the novel are Shelley's devoted study of science and alchemy. Other notable influences at work in the author that are discernable in *Frankenstein* are androgyny, atheism, and anti-government secret societies or fraternities—particularly the Bavarian Illuminati. Additionally, one cannot help recognizing the author's focused attention in developing characters whose traits revolve around their conflicting need for a soul mate while their actions undermine the possibility of a lasting relationship with their soul mate. The pilgrimage after Platonic love is frustrated by every male character and leads each of them to face the consequence: loss, rejection, abandonment, and isolation. There is a consistent psychological component running throughout the novel and one must ask how much of it is found in the inner conflicts of the author. Furthermore, *Frankenstein* is set against a backdrop of radical independence: first, a sailor embarking to an "uninhabited land," a paradise, holding answers to scientific mysteries; secondly, an alchemist-scientist determined to discover the principle of life while opposed by his contemporaries; and third, a creature whose superhuman abilities and indescribable nature are part of the sublime fabric woven into the story's backdrop.

Moreover, much might be argued from what is *not* evident

in the novel, i.e., intimate relationships between men and women, strong female characters, and the role of God. There is a glaring lack of fate or divine providence at work in the story of *Frankenstein*. Female characters in this novel are virtually unsubstantial shadows and passing vapors set against a rugged and sublime masculine environment in *Frankenstein*. In a curious fashion, this is a *manly* book to be sure, a novel—from start to finish—which unfolds from a uniquely masculine point of view, and note that the masculinity is distinctly such as the masculinity of Percy Shelley: unique! *Frankenstein* is not merely a middle-of-the-road masculine-leaning story, it is a specific *kind* of manliness that fills the pages, a distinctive androgynous, antisocial and independent sort of masculinity. It is not difficult to form an opinion about the person writing the story or identify the author's characteristic fingerprints in *Frankenstein*.

It should not come as any surprise that it was initially thought highly unlikely, if not impossible, that an eighteen-year-old *girl* was behind a story with such themes! Even modern feminist studies have had to wrestle with these problems, if not forced to preempt the internal inconsistencies of Mary Shelley as the author with their own creative solutions. Yet, today even the once anonymously written 1818 edition of *Frankenstein* bears the name of Mary Shelley as its author. Case closed.

There is no shortage of studies that can be found to support and analyze the authorship of *Frankenstein* by Mary Shelley. The argument *for* Mary Shelley as its author is relatively a non-argument in academic circles, and to raise a question concerning Mary Shelley as the author is to risk being labeled as a woman-hating troglodyte. What more needs to be said to end the brief and bewildering conversation concerning *Frankenstein*'s author than the very admission of Percy Shelley himself, that it was Mary and not he who wrote the novel? Why raise the question at all? By the time *Frankenstein* was released in its more popularly revised edition (1831), almost a decade after the death of Percy Shelley in 1822, the novel was no longer being published anonymously; it was printed with Mary Shelley's name as the author. As if to clear up any remaining confusion, Mary wrote an altogether new Preface for the book and gave a detailed account of how the book came to be written by her.

The question of authorship would seem to have been finally settled beyond any reasonable doubt, and yet, much like the name "Frankenstein," there still remain many confusing facts and inconsistencies in attributing the story to Mary Shelley. This book will argue that a case can be made that a serious misidentification has taken place regarding the author and demands a closer look. For that closer look we must begin with the anonymously written Preface to the 1818 edition and afterwards make a careful comparison to the Preface written in 1831.

THE PROBLEM WITH THE PREFACES
1818 PREFACE

A discerning and unprejudiced examination into the *Frankenstein* Prefaces will raise more than a few challenging questions, reveal several nagging inconsistencies, and cast serious doubts regarding Mary Shelley's authorship of *Frankenstein*. The Prefaces are as personal as fingerprints revealing the author's personality, his or her influences, education, and experiences. The Prefaces connect the author's life to the story, therefore one must expect that if a single author penned the 1818 edition and then revised his or her work a decade later, very little would change; the details would remain consistent. Yet it is precisely here in the section with the most personal evidence that the first red flags are raised for the careful reader. Consider first, the Preface to the 1818 Edition, the very edition which was published anonymously:

The event on which this fiction is founded has been supposed, by Dr. Darwin, and some of the physiological writers of Germany, as not of impossible occurrence. I shall not be supposed as according the remotest degree of serious faith to such an imagination; yet, in assuming it as the basis of a work of fancy, I have not considered myself as merely weaving a series of supernatural terrors. The event on which the interest of the story depends is exempt from the disadvantages of a mere tale of spectres or enchantment. It was recommended by the novelty of the situations which it develops; and, however impossible as a physical fact, affords a point of view to the imagination for the delineating of human passions more comprehensive and commanding than any which the ordinary relations of existing events can yield. [3]

The first paragraph of the Preface reveals an author who has far more than a passing familiarity with science; indeed the author is clearly endowed with an educated mind and inquisitive spirit that is dedicated to contemplating the deeper questions of science and human nature. The Preface reveals an author who has researched and been trained in rather advanced and esoteric material. He or she, according to the Preface, has been schooled in the writings and radical ideas of Erasmus Darwin (grandfather of the renowned scientist Charles Darwin) as well as the German physiologists.

ERASMUS DARWIN

Darwin's writings, including *The Botanic Garden* (1792), *Zoonomia* (1796), and in particular *The Temple of Nature* (1803), were profoundly inspirational to one person closely connected to *Frankenstein,* namely Percy Shelley—as early as 1811, at least seven years prior to the publication of *Frankenstein.*[4] Richard Holmes, in his biography *Shelley: The Pursuit,* writes that Darwin was "one of the archetypes of [Percy] Shelley's much admired eccentric scholars" and "Darwin's fusion of Science, philosophy, and poetry, was to prove an inspiration to Shelley."[5]

It is unquestionable that the emotions of human sympathy and loneliness expressed in Darwin's poetry were carried over into the traits associated with Frankenstein's creature—as well as experienced by Percy Shelley. Consider Darwin's Canto IV in the *Temple of Nature:*

> AND now, e'en I, whose verse reluctant sings
> The changeful state of sublunary things,
> Bend o'er Mortality with silent sighs,
> And wipe the secret tear-drops from my eyes,
> Hear through the night one universal groan,
> And mourn unseen for evils not my own,
> With restless limbs and throbbing heart complain,
> Stretch'd on the rack of sentimental pain![18]
> — Ah where can Sympathy reflecting find
> One bright idea to console the mind?
> One ray of light in this terrene abode
> To prove to Man the Goodness of his GOD?[6]

The words of Darwin are reminiscent of a man struggling to find a place in the world, sympathy with others, understanding, justice, meaning, and questioning the existence of God. The poetic themes found in Darwin are mirrored in the entire canon of Percy Bysshe Shelley's writings.

GERMAN PHYSIOLOGISTS

What of the German physiologists, whose influence, along with Darwin, were to be the threading that created the fabric from which *Frankenstein* was woven into a story? Few German physiologists are more notable than Albertus Magnus, the thirteenth-century Franciscan bishop, Doctor of the Catholic Church, and highly regarded philosopher. Albertus Magnus holds the rare distinction of claiming to have discovered the Philosopher's Stone, the elixir of life. This same Albertus Magnus, tradition claims, was a magician, alchemist, and the creator of an artificial human, a homunculus. The very same Albertus Magnus is explicitly mentioned in *Frankenstein* as one of three men to have been the early influence behind Victor Franken-stein's obsession to assemble a creature from dead parts and then animate it with new life—in short, to create another type of homun-culus. The key question is, what relationship, if any, exists between Albertus Magnus and Percy Shelley?

Newman Ivey White's monumental two-volume biography of Percy Bysshe Shelley reveals that between 1804 and 1809, while Shelley was still an adolescent studying at Eton,

> Shelley's scientific interests simply continued the enthusiasm for the mysteries and possibilities of Natural Science ... ranging from the physical to the metaphysical, he absorbed the scientific reveries of Albertus Magnus and Paracelsus with eager enthusi-asm for new sensation.[7]

Observe that the author of the original 1818 Preface is not *simply* weaving a series of "supernatural terrors" nor telling another "mere tale of spectres or enchantment," but explicitly stating scientific po-tentials. The author is proposing, through the literary genre of fic-tion, scientific ideas which were born of personal study, ideas which were the currency of modern advances in science. The author used a personal awareness of possibilities in science as the dock from which to embark into a philosophical sea of human uncertainties. The sto-ry has a supernatural element to it, perhaps even the feel of imitat-ing ghost stories from times past, but the author of the 1818 edition Preface wants the reader to be forewarned that this story is different! *Frankenstein* has a basis in *potential*; it is a scientific *possibility*, and therefore it is fiction embedded with a reasonable element of wonder because of the frightening potentials. In reality, this is *science* fiction, though the genre had not yet been attributed to any work of fiction at this time. *Frankenstein* is *science* fiction because the author was a per-son of science, dare we say a "man of science," who was well acquaint-ed with scientific advances and with the "men of science" of that time. This fact alone about the author should raise an eyebrow.

Carl Grabo, author, professor, scholar, and a foremost Percy

Bysshe Shelley authority, analyzed the writings of Shelley from the standpoint of how science influenced his poetry and prose. Grabo identified science as a key imprinted theme within Shelley's poetry. While Grabo conducted research for a book that he was writing as an analysis on the meaning of Shelley's profoundly difficult epic poem *Prometheus Unbound*, Grabo also determined that he would have to write another book solely dedicated to the subject of Shelley and the role of science. The second book was titled *A Newton Among Poets*.[8] In that book, Grabo states, "under slightly altered circumstances Shelley would have become a scientist"[9] and "the weight of evidence is too great, the consistency of Shelley's employment of scientific fact and theory too notable, to be denied."[10] For biographers of Percy Shelley this would come as little surprise; it was the study of science that took the greatest hold of young Percy Shelley when sent off as a child to Syon House and later to Eton.

In James Bieri's comprehensive biography *Percy Bysshe Shelley*, he describes how even in his childhood the influence of science began to form a foundation for Shelley's philosophy and writing:

> The lectures at Syon House on science and astronomy by the itinerant Dr. Adam Walker left an indelible imprint on Shelley. Walker, a science enthusiast and inventor, gave a series of vivid talks and demonstrations covering many scientific topics, as indicated by the title of his eighty-six-page pamphlet "Philosophy, viz. Magnetism, Mechanics, Chemistry, Pneumatics, Fortification, Optics, Use of Globes, etc., Astronomy." Fascinated with these lectures, Shelley probably heard them again at Eton, another of Walker's stops. Shelley's lifelong interest in chemistry, electricity, optics, and particularly astronomy infused his poetic imagery. Before leaving Syon House, when he was about twelve, Shelley began "scientific" experiments on his sisters and others at Field Place.[11]

Helen, Shelley's sister, describes the youthful Shelley as a Frankenstein in the making, an eccentric alchemist/scientist at the ripe age of twelve:

> When my brother commenced his studies in chemistry, and practiced electricity upon us, I confess my pleasure in it was entirely negatived by terror at its effects. Whenever he came to me with his piece of folded brown packing paper under his arm, and a bit of wire and a bottle ... my heart would sink with fear at his approach.[12]

Newman Ivey White adds to the picture of Percy Shelley's adolescent fascination with scientific experiments:

> He sent up fire-balloons, as other Eton boys were doing also. One Etonian represents Shelley's interest in explosives as extending to the purchase at auction of a brass cannon, which was captured by the tutors before it went into action... Shelley experimented with chemical brews and nearly blew himself up; he poisoned himself once. In confederation with Edward Leslie, he electrified a tom-cat. Striking higher, he even electrified "Butch" Bethell when that blundering tutor and landlord too hastily investigated a galvanic battery. At Field Place during vacations he was also demonstrating certain effects of powders and acids to his young sisters. He bought small electrical machines that were vended among the students by Adam Walker's assistant and with the aid of a traveling tinker he constructed a steam engine that duly exploded.[13]

Critically important in understanding the relationship of a scientific background necessary for the writing of *Frankenstein* and how it had a direct connection to the young Percy Shelley is the role of Doctor James Lind, Shelley's tutor at Eton. James Bieri describes Dr. Lind as a "latter-day Paracelsus" with an "apparatus-filled study" which "embodied Shelley's childhood fantasies..."[14] *The Journal of the Royal Society of Medicine* (May 2002) dedicated an article to the role of Dr. Lind, his influence in advances made in eighteenth-century science, and how these factors relate to the author of *Frankenstein:*

> ...doubts exist concerning Mary Shelley's degree of specific interest in, or knowledge of, scientific subjects. Accordingly, the level of influence exerted in this field by her husband, the poet Percy Bysshe Shelley, also remains open to debate. He maintained a keen interest in the world of natural philosophy, and many critics have noted the significance of the references to 'Dr. (Erasmus) Darwin and some of the physiological writers of Germany' in the novel's Preface... a closer examination of the medical themes running throughout the novel strongly suggests a more obscure influence at work, arising from Percy Shelley's friendship with a Scots doctor whilst he was still a schoolboy at Eton.
>
> During his last two years at Eton in 1809–1810, Percy Shelley became the friend of an elderly gentleman who was one of a number of persons approved by the school as suitable mentors for the boys.[15]

Astonishingly, Christopher Goulding, the article's author, has placed his finger on the very issue that not only reveals the writer of the Preface but also manages to pull back the veil and reveal *whose* knowledge and influence was at work in writing *Frankenstein.* In a bewildering fashion, however, Goulding maintains the role of Mary Shelley as the author of *Frankenstein,* a book dependent on a high degree of exposure and education in experimental science, which she did not have. Undoubtedly, it does require a tremendous effort to ignore the obvious—namely, the author of the novel is most likely to be the person who is already qualified in education and life experience: Percy Shelley.

Goulding continues,

Certain medical themes and quasi-autobiographical events in *Frankenstein* suggest the influence of Lind's character and work, via his pupil Percy Shelley. The description in the novel of Victor Frankenstein's medical studies at the University of Ingolstadt is an idealised version of Percy Shelley's scientific education, with the character Waldman, the chemistry lecturer, owing much to Lind. And an examination of Lind's own experiments reveals that he was even closer to the world of Frankenstein than has hitherto been acknowledged. Between 1782 and 1809, Lind maintained a regular correspondence with the London-based Italian physicist Tiberio Cavallo. Cavallo mentions Galvani's experiments on 19 June 1792, the year following publication of Galvani's research. On 11 July he asks Lind, 'Have you made any dead frogs jump like living ones?' And then on 15 August he writes, 'I am glad to hear of your success in the new experiments on muscular motion, and earnestly entreat you to prosecute them to the *ne plus ultra* of possible means.'[16]

With astonishing objectivity, *The Journal of the Royal Society of Medicine* supplies the obvious yet too often overlooked factual evidence that virtually guarantees the case for Percy's key role as the author of *Frankenstein*, via his education and life experience with Dr. Lind while at Eton:

Running alongside *Frankenstein*'s central plot concerning the creation of a monster, parallel themes address contemporary perceptions of the increasingly blurred boundary between life and death. These include an early excerpt where Victor Frankenstein is dragged freezing and emaciated aboard a ship from an ice floe in the Arctic Ocean:

'We accordingly brought him back to the deck, and restored him to animation by rubbing him with brandy, and forcing him to swallow a small quantity. As soon as he showed signs of life, we wrapped him up in blankets...'

Later, the creature attempts to resuscitate a young girl whose body he has dragged from a river: 'She was senseless; and I endeavoured, by every means in my power, to restore animation...'

Such references recall Lind's own medical education in Edinburgh under William Cullen, who was instrumental in the early codification of procedures for the revival of drowned or otherwise asphyxiated persons. Cullen is, in fact, mentioned within this context in a medical work known to have been ordered by Percy Shelley from his bookseller in July 1812. Robert Thornton's *Medical Extracts* includes a lengthy passage on methods suitable for persons being 'recalled to life' from 'the silent mansions of the tomb,' and mentions the theories of Cullen and Boerhaave on the causes of death from asphyxiation by hanging. Interestingly, Waldman's assessment in *Frankenstein* of modern philosophers as the successors to the alchemists bears similarities to comments in Thornton's book. Lind's interest in forensic medicine may be seen as the inspiration for Percy Shelley's creation of perhaps the earliest example of ratiocinative detective drama in his play *The Cenci*, and his influence can be found in other of Shelley's themes.[17]

Finally, despite the clear objective proof set forward, analyzed, and effectively proving the case for Percy Shelley as the author of *Frankenstein*, Goulding stops short of taking the next step. One might argue that Goulding's final deduction is contrary to every point of fact he outlined. Yet, in fairness to Goulding, he is not alone as a scholar whose valuable research simply cannot make the logical step toward Percy Shelley's authorship of *Frankenstein*. One can only conclude that there is an unconscious—if not irrational—blindness on the part of many in academia due to the celebrity status of Mary Shelley as the accepted author. Goulding writes,

It is also fascinating to consider how his [Lind's] ideas, mediated through Percy Shelley and others, worked on Mary Shelley's imagination.[18]

And thus the authorship of Mary Shelley remains safely entrenched and guarded by attributing Percy Shelley with supplying his future wife with *imagination*!

However, the facts are simple. It was Dr. Lind who trained, educated, and encouraged Shelley to pursue his studies in natural and physical sciences, chemical and electrical experimentation, and to continue in the writings of Albertus Magnus and Paracelsus. It was Dr. Lind who exposed Percy Shelley to a laboratory environment where Lind had constructed an earthquake machine, an anemometer, and a "thunder house" for studying Franklin's lightning rod. Additionally, according to James Bieri, it was also Dr. Lind who suggested using electricity to cure insanity and, possibly for influencing a key idea in *Frankenstein*, to employ electrical stimulation to animate dead frogs. Coincidentally, being a friend of Captain James Cook, Lind accompanied Sir Joseph Banks on the Royal Society Iceland expedition of 1772.[19]

Shelley's years at Eton (1805–1809) only furthered his eccentricities in the use of electrical machines, chemical apparatus, and studies in the relationship of science to human nature. Dr. Lind was the guide to young Shelley, an extraordinary guide for an extraordinary student, a student who would turn his life studies and experiences into an autobiographical science fiction narrative.

If the anonymous author of the 1818 edition of Frankenstein was writing the Preface from the perspective of personal education, interest, and experience, the evidence within the first paragraph of the Preface alone is overwhelmingly indicative of the hand of Percy Bysshe Shelley as its author.

Let us now consider the second paragraph in the Preface to the 1818 first edition and anonymously written Frankenstein:

> I have thus endeavoured to preserve the truth of the elementary principles of human nature, which I have not scrupled to innovate upon their combinations. The *Iliad*, the tragic **poetry of Greece — Shakespeare**, in the *Tempest* and *Midsummer Night's*

Dream, — and most especially **Milton**, in *Paradise Lost*, conform to this rule; and the most humble novelist, who seeks to confer or receive amusement from his labours, may, without presumption, apply to prose fiction a licence, or rather a rule, from the adoption of which so many exquisite combinations of human feeing have resulted in the highest specimens of poetry.[xxv]

The second paragraph, like the first, is revealing. Moving from Darwin and German physiologists to the writings of Shakespeare, Milton, and the poets of Greece, the anonymous author of the 1818 edition of *Frankenstein* has indicated another area of his or her education, personal interest, and experience. At first reading it might be argued that Mary Shelley was exposed to such literature from a young age, being the daughter of a highly regarded author, William Godwin. Her own journals describe her as a reader from a young age and exposed to many of the classics, thus perhaps it is too much to argue that this second paragraph from the Preface leans in favor of Percy any more than toward Mary Shelley. Yet, there is one important literary connection that throws the weight for Percy quite over the top in this second paragraph, and it comes from the Preface of Percy Shelley's epic poem *Prometheus Unbound*.

The imagery which I have employed will be found in many instances to have been drawn from the operations of the human mind, or from those external actions by which they are expressed. This is unusual in modern Poetry; although Dante and **Shakespeare** are full of instances of the same kind: Dante indeed more than any other poet and with greater success. But the **Greek poets**, as writers to whom no resource of awakening the sympathy of their contemporaries was unknown, were in the habitual use of this power...We owe **Milton** to the progress and development of the same spirit... if this similarity be the result of imitation, I am willing to confess that I have imitated.[21]

Notice that the author of the 1818 edition *Frankenstein* Preface *as well as* the author of the poem *Prometheus Unbound* admits that he or she is not entirely original, is not an innovator, but relies upon the product of past minds, geniuses who tapped into human emotions or feelings through their words. Specifically Shakespeare, Milton, and the Greek poets are mentioned in *both* the *Frankenstein* Preface as well as *Prometheus Unbound* which was written by *Percy Shelley*. It is not coincidental, not merely similar, but as sure an intellectual fingerprint as ever might be found in literature when comparing two works of fiction: The Preface to *Frankenstein, or the Modern Prometheus* was written by the same author as the Preface to the epic poem *Prometheus Unbound*; that author is Percy Shelley.

The third paragraph of the anonymously written 1818 first edition of *Frankenstein* only confirms this conclusion by offering a few more interesting facts worthy of consideration:

The circumstances on which **my story rests** was suggested in casual conversation. It was commenced, partly as a source of amusement, and partly as an expedient for exercising any untried resources of mind. Other motives were mingled with these, as the work proceeded. I am by no means indifferent to the manner in which whatever moral tendencies exist in the sentiments of characters it contains shall affect the reader; yet my chief concern in this respect has been limited to the avoiding the enervating effects of the novels of the present day, and the exhibition of the amiableness of domestic affection, and the excellence of universal virtue. The opinions which naturally spring from the character and situation of the hero are by no means to be conceived as existing always in my own conviction; nor is any inference justly to be drawn from the following pages as prejudicing any philosophical doctrine of whatever kind.[22]

Given the previous evidence already presented, it is worthy of notice that the Preface is written as much in terms of autobiography as by way of exposition concerning the text which is to follow in the novel. For instance, notice the wording in the previous paragraph, "*the circumstances on which* **my story** *rests ...*" an obvious, though easy to overlook, association linking the story itself to the author of the Preface; **this point will be very important to keep in mind**.

There is also within the third paragraph of the Preface a curious attempt given by the author to distance himself or herself from any moral, immoral, or philosophical doctrines which could be construed to promote behavior or beliefs suggested in the story, noticeably such damnable ideas as: creation without the hand of God; incest between cousins—or brother and sister as Victor and Elizabeth related to one another; bigamy; scientific experimentation usurping the moral limits of society; or even revolution, a dangerous idea that could be easily interpreted by setting the creature's birth in the city of Ingolstadt, home of the Bavarian Illuminati.

Such a disclaimer as is made in the third paragraph of the Preface certainly adds intrigue. Although the author would have the reader believe that he or she does not promote any philosophy nor is attempting to uphold or cast down any universal virtues, the Preface is actually baiting the reader, implanting ideas, and at the same time trying to deny any intention for such an agenda. It is subversive, calculated, misleading, and precisely fitting into the pattern of Percy Bysshe Shelley, who had a long record of writing subversive papers anonymously or with a pseudonym, denying any part in the propagation of the work, and yet clearly using every trick in a secret society playbook to accomplish his purpose while maintaining a covert position.

Consider as one dot to connect—and a strangely familiar theme touched upon in the novel *Frankenstein*—that Shelley's calculated misdirection and use of anonymity was previously used by him to argue *for a belief system* of human morality without the need of a Creator; and he did so while outwardly denying his real purpose.

As a student at the University of Oxford, Percy Shelley wrote *The Necessity of Atheism* (1811), an anonymous tract which he not only distributed to the heads of all Oxford colleges but also sent to all of the bishops and select priests in the Church of England. Such intellectual effrontery in executing such a plan while attending an institution—the University of Oxford—which required an oath of faith is evidence of a self-confident covert revolutionary who assumed that he could pull it off and remain unknown as the originator of the tract! In addition to writing the tract, he followed it up with more anti-religious writings designed to be even more misleading. Shelley could not resist a letter campaign using a pseudonym, attempting to draw Anglican clergymen, in essence baiting them, into discussions concerning the same anonymous tract as if he was the one having a crisis of faith after reading the brilliant tract that he himself wrote![23]

The *modus operandi* is identical: choose a controversial theme—one of his favorites, atheism; hide behind anonymity; deny responsibility for the work, and if necessary, write letters pointing those who might suspect his hand in the work to the name of another *actual* person or substituting a false name.[24] To what purpose? Percy Bysshe Shelley did not seek his name in the spotlight nor expect his fame to come to him with recognition and financial gain; rather he worked from behind the curtain to pull off his intellectual and behavioral revolution. Denial of his own work, misdirection, and distancing himself from his own opinions were constants in Shelley's life. This third paragraph of the Preface actually acts as another proof of his work rather than suggest the hand of anyone else. He wrote, denied his writings, attributed them to another, and kept his head low when or if the bullets began to fly.

And finally, the last two paragraphs of the 1818 *Frankenstein* Preface are essential pieces to examine with a critical eye for specific historic details. These final paragraphs in the First Edition Preface, set beside the *curiously* new narrative crafted by Mary for her 1831 Preface, will build a solid case of evidence tampering as it pertains to authorship. If, as is being argued here, Percy Bysshe Shelley is the author of the 1818 anonymous Preface and novel, the details of how the book came to be written might well have had to be altered in order to take a subtle turn away from him and his purposes once the book was later attributed to another person, namely Mary. When she released the 1831 revised edition of *Frankenstein* she had to present it as if *both* editions were her own work. And now, the last two paragraphs of the 1818 Preface:

> It is a subject also of additional interest to the author, that this story was begun in the majestic region where the scene is principally laid and in society which cannot cease to be regretted. I passed the summer of 1816 in the environs of Geneva. The season was cold and rainy, and in the evenings we crowded around a blazing wood fire, and occasionally amused ourselves with some German stories of ghosts, which happened to fall into our hands. These tales excited in us a playful desire of imitation. Two other friends (a tale from the pen of one of whom would be far more acceptable to the public than any thing I can ever hope to produce) and myself agreed to write each a story, founded on some supernatural occurrence.
>
> The weather, however, suddenly became serene; and my two friends left me on a journey among the Alps, and lost, in the magnificent scenes which they present, all memory of their ghostly visions. The following tale is the only one which has been completed. [25]

The details in these two paragraphs need to be considered carefully. Pay careful attention to the fact that the occasion on which this story was initiated came about when the author, along with *two* friends, "agreed to write each a story, founded on some supernatural occurrence." In total, there are *three* persons present—the Preface writer and the other two friends. No more, no less. Who were they? Taking a clue from the Preface that "a tale from the pen of one of whom would be far more acceptable to the public than any thing I can ever hope to produce," it is logical to assume that *Frankenstein*'s author is referring to none other than Lord Byron, with whom much of the 1816 stormy summer was spent in Switzerland at Byron's Villa Diodati estate.

By 1816 Lord Byron was a celebrity whose poetry and life made him both famous and scandalous, and unquestionably England's most popular poet. He had already published the first two cantos of *Childe Harold's Pilgrimage,* and the Byronic hero awakened the public's love affair with Lord Byron. Thus, by a simple process of elimination, the *Frankenstein* author was *one* of the three present during the time of the "agreement" and the *second* person had to be Lord Byron.

Curiously, the Preface writer suggests that his or her work would be by comparison less "acceptable" to the public. If the argument for Percy Shelley as the author holds true, this would make perfect sense as Shelley was a well-known figure in England for all of the wrong reasons: he was an acknowledged atheist; had been cast out of the University of Oxford for his role in having written *The Necessity of Atheism*; had run off with two of William Godwin's adolescent children (Mary and Claire Clairmont) while he was already married; and was considered a young revolutionary.

Four years earlier Shelley had anonymously published several anti-government writings, including *A Letter to Lord Ellenborough*, which not only argued for freedom of the press but specifically for the right to publish material even if was atheistic. The same year as the *Ellenborough letter*, 1812, Shelley had published *The Devil's Walk*, a poem condemning the British government, the "brainless" King, and the Anglican Church. Percy Shelley protested the harsh economic conditions and shortage of food which was causing great suffering among the poor, and placed blame squarely on the authorities as acting in the very nature of Satan. From this time onward, perhaps even sooner, Percy Shelley was under surveillance from the government.[26] In further Illuminati-style covert and subversive manner, Shelley's manner of distributing his seditious literature was to send them to sea in corked bottles, launch them in hot air balloons, and place them in miniature flotillas at sea.[27] Finally, and not so coincidentally as it relates to Shelley's role in *Frankenstein*, he had written to his liberal publisher at this time, Thomas Hookham, Jr., requesting approx-

LORD BYRON   JOHN WILLIAM POLIDORI

imately seventy books, including Davy's recently published book on chemistry, Thornton's *Medical Extracts* which concerned reviving drowning victims, and Paracelsus' influence on modern chemistry.[28] It is nearly impossible to find a single moment in Shelley's adult life when revolution, atheism, alchemy, and anonymity were not squarely intertwined and being used in his writings.

And yet, is it possible that Mary Shelley was the one whose writing would be far less "acceptable" to the public than Lord Byron's? If one argues that a young girl's writings would be less acceptable than Lord Byron's, that goes without saying; however, consider what a weak argument it is by comparison! Is that *all* the anonymous author of the 1818 *Frankenstein* Preface meant? Surely not.

A final question lingers: who was the third person present when the decision was agreed upon to write a story "founded on some supernatural occurrence"? The choices are limited to the names recorded in the journals which were kept that stormy Switzerland summer in 1816: John William Polidori, Lord Byron's twenty-eight-year-old physician and struggling writer; Claire Clairmont, Mary's eighteen-year-old stepsister; or Mary Shelley herself, if indeed Percy Bysshe is the author of the 1818 edition Preface and novel *Frankenstein.*

The answer is supplied, though the problem is not entirely resolved, by the journal of John William Polidori who wrote that "the ghost-stories are begun by all but me."[29] Therefore, *Frankenstein*'s author and the writer of the Preface in 1818, Lord Byron, and assumedly John William Polidori, are the most likely three placed together when the decision is made to write their supernatural stories. What of Mary?

1831 PREFACE — MARY THE DECEIVER *or* THE CO-CONSPIRATOR?

It is not necessary to examine each paragraph, sentence, and word in the 1831 Preface in order to make a case of inconsistencies, or even of a hoax being perpetrated, and a change of hands on the text between 1818 and 1831. The first and most necessary point of fact is that there is no question whatsoever who wrote the 1831 Preface; it was Mary Shelley. Percy Bysshe Shelley had died in 1822 and therefore ruling him out is quite simple. What is necessary to observe is the inconsistency between the two Prefaces as well as one *very important* admission made by Mary in her 1831 Preface, but more on that later.

Mary Shelley's Preface (1831) tells a very similar tale, though with some glaring inconsistencies. Observe:

> In the summer of 1816, we visited Switzerland, and became the neighbours of Lord Byron. At first we spent our pleasant hours on the lake, or wandering on its shores; ...but it proved a wet, ungenial summer, and incessant rain often confined us for days to the house. Some volumes of ghost stories, translated from the German into French, fell into our hands... 'We will each write a ghost story,' said Lord Byron; and his proposition was acceded to. There were **four** of us.[30] [emphasis added]

Suddenly another member of the party has been added on the occasion of the decision to write the ghost stories. Is this an oversight? A correction in memory? Or is this a necessary, albeit fabricated, revision in order to make sense of Mary Shelley's role as the author? Consider three alternatives:

1.) *If* only three were present on this occasion, as stated in the 1818 version, and *if* those three were Percy Shelley, Lord Byron, and John Polidori, clearly the most logical three among the five present, it hardly makes sense that an excluded fourth person who was a teenage mistress of Percy Shelley would be so bold as to write her own *unsolicited* story. This alternative is unacceptable.

2.) *If* only three were present on this occasion as stated in the 1818 version, and *if* those three were Lord Byron, *Mary Shelley*, and William Polidori, it would leave many *Frankenstein* readers as well as all historians wondering how it could be that Percy Bysshe Shelley, a very accomplished author of prose fiction and poetry, would be excluded in such a gathering, particularly as he and Lord Byron were virtually inseparable! Furthermore, it would open up more than a few nagging questions as to where he was when such a wonderfully challenging literary event was taking shape. This alternative is doomed as well. Percy Shelley must have been present and in the gathering.

3.) *If* only three were present on this occasion as stated in the 1818 version, and *if* those three were Lord Byron, Mary Shelley, and Percy Bysshe Shelley, what is the reader to make of the fact that John Polidori records the same event in his journal and completed a story, *The Vampyre*, which by his own account was written on this occasion? Many readers in 1831 were aware of the fact that Polidori published his story in 1819, therefore it simply defies reason to exclude Polidori from the ghost-story event.

Thus, in order to fabricate the elaborate hoax of Mary Shelley's authorship, the solution was simple: the events must be changed! The reader is now left with the obvious answer as to why Mary Shelley was obligated to revise the number of people present during the ghost-story event, and yet somehow Claire Clairmont, Mary's stepsister and the future mother of Byron's child, is left out of the revised history concerning this moment. Why not just throw in one more name? One wonders if this was an accidental oversight or if it was Mary Shelley's not-so-gentle revenge on Claire for her ongoing affair with Percy Bysshe Shelley. Either way, the 1831 Preface has now accommodated Mary Shelley at the literary moment when *Frankenstein* was birthed by Byron's suggestion.

Mary Shelley continues her 1831 Preface with some additionally unknown details which are worthy of notice:

> The noble author began a tale, a fragment of which he printed at the end of his poem of Mazeppa. Shelley, more apt to embody ideas and sentiments in the radiance of brilliant imagery, and in the music of the most melodious verse that adorns our language, than to invent the machinery of a story, commenced one founded on the experiences of his early life. Poor Polidori had some terrible idea about a skull-headed lady ... the illustrious poets also, annoyed by the platitude of prose, speedily relinquished their uncongenial task. I busied myself to think of a story, —a story to rival those which had excited us to this task. One which would speak to the mysterious fears of our nature, and awaken thrilling horror—one to make the reader dread to look round, to curdle the blood, and quicken the beatings of the heart. I thought and pondered—vainly. I felt that blank incapability of invention which is the greatest misery of authorship, when dull Nothing replies to our anxious invocations *Have you thought of a story?* I was asked each morning, and each morning I was forced to reply with a mortifying negative.[31]

Note what we now have. First, from Mary Shelley's revised Preface we learn that the other authors, namely Shelley, Byron, and Polidori, failed to live up to the challenge or simply just gave up due to their lack of interest in prose as opposed to poetry. Apparently *"poor Polidori"* also was mistaken in his account that everyone *except* him was writing their stories. This second mistake in this 1831 Preface is one of factual detail; it was not Polidori but rather *Mary*

Shelley who was fabricating an entirely new series of events around which she would insert herself as a heroic author struggling against her lack of imagination in a room blessed with that "noble author" (Byron) and the apt and brilliant Shelley who writes with "music of the most melodious verse" that adorns the English language.

Another misleading fact is the explicit statement that the poet Percy Shelley found prose to be an annoyance. The fact is that Shelley's literary output already included a considerable amount of material other than poetry, including two earlier novels: *Zastrozzi*, which he wrote in 1809 and which was published in 1810 anonymously with the initials PBS; and also *St. Irvyne, or the Rosicrucian*, which was published in 1811 anonymously by "A Gentleman of the University of Oxford." The glaring truth is that Percy Bysshe Shelley was a twice-published novelist prior to *Frankenstein* and that his method of writing anonymously had not changed, nor had his intention to write fictional novels without drawing attention to himself at the time of *Frankenstein*.

And finally, a glimmer of reality breaks through the charade when Mary confesses that Shelley wrote, or at least started, his story "founded on the experiences of his early life." The confession of this truth is critical and easily established by the details we will consider within the story of *Frankenstein*. But according to Mary Shelley he "relinquished the uncongenial task" due to his annoyance with writing prose. What was relinquished by Percy Shelley was his desire to be associated directly as the author of *Frankenstein*, and yet his association cannot be ignored as the novel actually reveals the experiences of his life. Mary, acting under and with the fullest cooperation of Percy, attempted to gloss over his role as author by writing a new Preface, putting her own gloss on the events, fabricating facts, and claiming the story as her own in an effort designed to steer the readers away from the belief that Shelley was interested in completing the annoying task. The co-conspirator in this hoax was indeed Mary Shelley.

MARY SHELLEY

As Mary Shelley's revised history unfolds, a familiar story re-emerges, one similar to that which is found in the 1818 Preface:

> Many and long were the conversations between Lord Byron and Shelley, to which I was a devout but nearly silent listener. During one of these, various philosophical doctrines were discussed, and among others the nature of the principle of life, and whether there was any possibility of its ever being discovered and communicated. They talked of the experiments of Dr. Darwin ... [32]

The change is subtle but considerable: Mary is the novice, the learner, the silent disciple who must rely on the expertise of others to fill in the gaps of her academic shortcomings. She is not the one well versed in Darwin. She is not the radical young student studying the writings of Paracelsus and Albertus Magnus, or any other German physiologist. She is, in essence, a fly on the wall attempting to pull in as much information as possible in order to use it in the future. Although the Preface accounts sound similar, the difference is monumental and demonstrates what has already been established, namely, *Frankenstein* is the product of one who was steeped in science, rubbed shoulders with the men of science, carried on his own experiments at home and in school with friends, family, and wandering animals. The 1818 Preface makes absolute sense when placed within the context of an author who was educated, experienced, and influenced in the fields which set the background for *Frankenstein*. It makes perfect sense if the author is Percy and not Mary Shelley.

If it were not for the necessity of maintaining Shelley's hoax, the following sentences penned by Mary Shelley in her 1831 Preface would be remembered in history as among the greatest lies ever committed to ink, one of the worst betrayals committed against another person, the Judas kiss from a novice scribbler to a master poet, for it is an atrociously evil distortion of reality, one which highly suggests how deeply Mary Shelley understood her husband's desire to remain anonymous:

At first I thought but of a few pages—of a short tale; but Shelley urged me to develope [sic] the idea at greater length. I certainly did not owe the suggestion of one incident, nor scarcely of one train of feeling, to my husband, and yet but for his incitement, it would never have taken the form in which it was presented to the world.[33]

How can this be? Had Mary Shelley taken complete leave of her senses? Only mere sentences prior to these bewildering statements she has identified that it was in the course of hearing her husband discuss concepts of reanimation, the use of galvanism in modern science, and the writings and experiments of Erasmus Darwin, that she was moved to consider such a subject for her novel. Now, in the midst of remembering with clarity exactly how the book came to her more than a decade earlier, she cannot think of anything whatsoever, not even a train of feeling, which she owes to Percy Shelley. All evidence—even that which is presented by the most committed Mary Shelley scholars who defend her singular genius as the author of *Frankenstein,* but who must admit that the *Frankenstein* manuscript corrections were written in Percy Shelley's own hand—proves that he was more than just the fellow who merely "urged" her to turn a short story into a novel! If ever a gross understatement was written, surely it was when Mary Shelley wrote, *"I certainly did not owe the suggestion of one incident, nor scarcely of one train of feeling, to my husband."*

Considering that Mary was well aware of who wrote *Frankenstein,* and the nonsensical inaccuracy of such statements by her, it must be admitted that she greatly overstated her independent role as the author in order to secure the credibility of her authorship and likewise maintain Percy's wish to be anonymous. A second, though highly unlikely, possibility is that her father, William Godwin, had more than a small part himself in the revision to the Preface of 1831 and did everything he could to make sure that his former son-in-law was never discovered as the author of *Frankenstein,* thus guaranteeing his daughter's fame and the potential monetary gain which he was always seeking to take out of the hand of Percy Shelley. In Shelley's death William Godwin may have finally found a way to reach deeper into the pocket of the man who eloped with his only natural daughter. The insurmountable problem with this theory is that it leads to the inevitable conclusion that if Mary did not co-conspire with Percy to hide his name from *Frankenstein*, she in fact *did* betray him and has stained her integrity beyond repair. This theory I find to be entirely out of character with Mary and therefore dismiss it.

And now for the moment when the curtain is pulled back and the truth is finally revealed. Mary confesses,

> From this declaration I must except the preface. As far as I can recollect, *it was entirely written by him*.[34] [emphasis added]

Were it not so obvious from the accumulation of facts presented in the 1818 Preface, this revelation might come as a surprise. All that is lacking is the final confession that the same man (yes, *man*) who wrote the 1818 first edition Preface for *Frankenstein* was also the author of the novel, just as he described himself in the preface with the words, "*my* story ..."

For a comparative reading of the two Prefaces, see Appendix A.

1 Mary Shelley, *Frankenstein, or the Modern Prometheus*, J. Paul Hunter, ed., *The Original 1818 Text Norton Critical Edition* (W.W. Norton and Co.: 1996), p. 5

2 Cf. *Transhumanism: A Grimoire of Alchemical Agendas* (2012) by Joseph P. Farrell and Scott D. de Hart for a more detailed analysis of manimals and the alchemical agenda behind some modern advances in science.

3 Ibid., p. 5

4 Richard Holmes, *Shelley: The Pursuit* (E.P. Dutton & Co.: 1975), p. 75

5 Ibid., 75

6 Erasmus Darwin, *The Temple of Nature*, Canto IV, cf. www.english.upenn.edu/Projects/knarf/Darwin/temple4.html

7 Newman Ivey White, *Shelley* (Alfred A. Knopf: 1940) Vol. 1, pp. 40–42

8 Carl Grabo, *A Newton Among Poets: Shelley's Use of Science in Prometheus Unbound* (University of North Carolina Press: 1930), p. vii. Grabo writes, "The material of this book was planned as a part of the notes to an edition of *Prometheus Unbound* now in preparation. The scientific citations proved, however, to be so extensive and the need for sketching Shelley's background so evident, that is independent publication was decided upon."

9 Ibid., p. 3

10 Ibid., p. xi

11 James Bieri, *Percy Bysshe Shelley: A Biography* (Johns Hopkins University Press: 2008), p. 50

12 Ibid., p. 50

13 White, vol. 1, pp. 40–41

14 Bieri, p. 65

15 Christopher Goulding, *The Royal Society of Medicine* (May 2002), cf. textualities.net/christopher-goulding/the-real-dr-frankenstein

16 Ibid.

17 Ibid.

18 Ibid.

19 Bieri, p. 66

20 Mary Shelley, *Frankenstein, or the Modern Prometheus*, J. Paul Hunter, ed., *The Original 1818 Text Norton Critical Edition* (W.W. Norton and Co.: 1996), p. 5 (emphasis added)

21 Percy Bysshe Shelley, *Shelley's Poetry and Prose*, The Preface to *Prometheus Unbound,* eds., Donald Reiman and Neil Fraistat (W.W. Norton & Co.: 2002), pp. 207–208 (emphasis added)

22 Mary Shelley, *Frankenstein, or the Modern Prometheus*, J. Paul Hunter, ed., *The Original 1818 Text Norton Critical Edition* (W.W. Norton and Co.: 1996), pp. 5–6

23 Bieri, p. 104

24 Shelley was known to have used names of friends, i.e. Medwin, and the mailing addresses of friends, to mislead his captive audience. There are few instances when Shelley actually wrote controversial literature and dared to expose himself as the author. Typically, Shelley used the names of acquaintances or pseudonyms in order to publish or write provocative letters.

25 Mary Shelley, *Frankenstein, or the Modern Prometheus*, J. Paul Hunter, ed., *The Original 1818 Text Norton Critical Edition* (W.W. Norton and Co.: 1996), p. 6

26 Shelley, in writing to his publisher, Hookham, suggested that his controversial literature might be shown to "any friends who *are not informers*" because of "knowledge I now possess" including fear of government prosecution and of being under surveillance." Bieri, pp. 216–217

27 Bieri, pp. 217–218

28 Ibid., p. 217

29 William Michael Rossetti, ed., *The Diary of Dr. John William Polidori, 1816, Relating to Byron, Shelley, etc.* (Elkin Matthew, 1911), p. 125

30 Mary Shelley, *Frankenstein, or the Modern Prometheus*, J. Paul Hunter, ed., *The Original 1818 Text Norton Critical Edition* (W.W. Norton and Co.: 1996), p. 170

31 Ibid., p. 171

32 Ibid., p. 171

33 Ibid., p. 172

34 Ibid., p. 173

CHAPTER 2

SHELLEY, THE ALCHEMIST

I see by your eagerness, and the wonder and hope which your eyes
express, my friend, that you expect to be informed of the secret with
which I am acquainted; that cannot be ...

— Victor Frankenstein,
Frankenstein, or the Modern Prometheus, 1818 1ˢᵗ Edition
Anonymous [1]

Nearly every great ghost story begins on a dark night, wind whistling through the trees, rain pelting the windows, lightning streaking across the sky, and an image appearing as a shadow in the darkness peering through a window. So it is with *Frankenstein* as Mary Shelley beckons the reader to imagine how the creature came to her in a waking dream:[2]

> When I placed my head on my pillow, I did not sleep, nor could I
> be said to think. My imagination, unbidden, possessed and guid-
> ed me, gifting the successive images that arose in my mind with
> a vividness far beyond the usual bounds of reverie...I need only
> describe the spectre which had haunted my midnight pillow. On
> the morrow I announced that I had thought of a story. I began
> that day with the words, It was on a dreary night of November,
> making only a transcript of the grim terrors of my waking dream.

The history behind *Frankenstein,* as written by Mary Shelley in her 1831 Preface, as we have previously noted, is almost as legendary as the novel itself. Few books have so memorable a history, and perhaps this is the primary reason why so few scholars have been willing to consider an alternative origin for *Frankenstein.* Reconsider the cinematic quality of the backstory: a stormy summer in Switzerland; a small band of poets—including Lord Byron—and a couple of young girls in a candlelit room; a blazing fire of orange and yellow reflected in the eyes of literary rebels reading German ghost stories; talk of the living dead; eccentric scientists with electrical devices; and a young girl's waking dream of a spectre. This is pure Hollywood gold in terms of setting up the occasion for a ghost story to end all ghost stories! One might almost imagine that the backstory is as fictional as the creature sewn together from dead tissue and brought to life as a murderous demon.

Mary Shelley's dramatic 1831 Preface gives the reader precisely what any reader would desire and in so doing she has written a clever cover story and pulled off a skilled act of misdirection, but *to what end?* While the reader is focused on the creature stirring in the shadows of Mary Shelley's waking dream, Percy Bysshe Shelley magically disappears from the stormy summer in Switzerland. A literary sleight of hand has effectively removed even the least possibility of linking the name of Percy Bysshe Shelley to the authorship of *Frankenstein*:

I certainly did not owe the suggestion of one incident, nor scarcely of one train of feeling, to my husband.[3]

Mary Shelley's disclaimer concerning her husband's participation with *Frankenstein* is explicit, all-encompassing, and oddly reminiscent of the disclaimer found at the end of motion pictures:

All characters appearing in this work are fictitious. Any resemblance to real persons, living or dead, is purely coincidental.

Not surprisingly, the motion picture disclaimer originated under circumstances in which the characters appearing in the work do *in fact* bear an uncanny resemblance to real persons.[4] Mary Shelley's attempt to remain true to her husband's hoax and to shield him from notice as the author could not overcome one major obstacle, namely that of Shelley himself, who bore an undeniable resemblance to characters in *Frankenstein*. Such an insincere disclaimer in the 1831 Preface should be seen as the most sure indication that those who seek for Percy Bysshe Shelley shall indeed find him.

PERCY BYSSHE SHELLEY, AUTHOR OF FRANKENSTEIN (LEFT)
FRANKENSTEIN'S "MONSTER" AS PORTRAYED BY BORIS KARLOFF5

In Richard Holmes' biography *Shelley: The Pursuit*, the author writes, "implicitly, Shelley accepted his own identification as Frankenstein's monster."[6] Holmes' astute observation that Shelley is virtually one and the same with the creature, and that Shelley himself was aware of this fact, nearly defies reason at the point that the author then is incapable or unwilling to accept the reason why a main character is so perfect a literary sketch of Mary's husband. One wonders why any scholar would be fooled by Mary's disclaimer after actually reading *Frankenstein,* the story of an intelligent, isolated, Illuminati-influenced, incestuous young man and student of alchemy whose tutoring in scientific method leads him to envision a world of men without the need of God. Indeed, Holmes was very near the truth when he wrote, "Shelley was well aware of the many autobiographical influences which shaped Mary's book."[7]

THE YOUNG ALCHEMIST

Frankenstein is *not* a horror story. This observation is so self-evident that, as we have previously written, the entire 1831 Preface has been called into question. Although Mary Shelley hoped to mis-direct the readers of her 1831 Preface to think of *Frankenstein* as a waking dream of horrific spectres and a contest-winning ghost sto-ry, there was one person who understood and explained the real un-derlying purpose of *Frankenstein:* the man who anonymously wrote it, Percy Bysshe Shelley.

> In this the direct moral of the book consists; and it is perhaps the most important, and of the most universal application, of any moral that can be enforced by example. Treat a person ill, and he will be-come wicked. Requite affection with scorn; —let one being be se-lected, for whatever cause, as the refuse of his kind—divide him, a social being, from society, and you impose upon him the irresistible obligations—malevolence and selfishness. It is thus that, too often in society, those who are best qualified to be its benefactors and its ornaments, are branded by some accident with scorn, and changed, by neglect and solitude of heart, into a scourge and a curse.[8]

So wrote Percy Bysshe Shelley in 1817 in what would remain an unpublished review of *Frankenstein* until 1832 when Shelley's cous-in Thomas Medwin presented it for publication in *The Athenaeum.* The novel, according to Shelley himself, is an indictment against the authoritarian structures in society which use threat, abuse, punish-ment, and separation or isolation to force obedience and conformi-ty. It is an indictment against the supposed God who created man "in His image" and then terrorized and punished man for his unique nature as a rational independent person. It is an indictment against the God who established boundaries for human society, first in mar-riage and the family, and then extended into communities, and from those communities arose tyrannous governments and abusive reli-gious institutions. While much more will be said regarding Shelley's religious views and how they are embedded in *Frankenstein*, what is critical to observe at this point is that *Frankenstein* is not a ghost sto-ry written to frighten readers with images of fantastic monsters. It is a treatise with a purpose; a story of man's aspirations and society's disapproval; *Frankenstein* is an autobiographical novel inspired by the thoughts and experiences of its author, Percy Bysshe Shelley.

Frankenstein is a series of life stories, narratives weaved together for a common theme. One such narrative is that of an alchemist turned scientist who seeks to offer an alternative to an upside-down and unenlightened world, whose expertise in science unlocks the alchemical goal of transforming the base material of undignified human flesh into a new man, a higher man, a second Adam. Paradise revisited in the garden of Ingolstadt. Frankenstein's creature is abandoned into a world without love, without compassion, a world of people made in the image of its god. The creature, a stranger and foreigner to this world, must learn how to survive alone in a world without another being who is comparable to it or compatible with it. A new man for a new society, and a new world order created by the hands of an enlightened man— this is the story of *Frankenstein*! The question then arises: if the story does not originate in the waking dream of Mary Shelley, where does the story of the alchemist turned scientist and creator originate? To answer that question is to return to the childhood of Percy Bysshe Shelley. Newman Ivey White, Shelley's biographer, accurately wrote, "Of few writers more than Shelley can it be said that his works are the man himself."[9]

FRANKENSTEIN AND SHELLEY THE ALCHEMIST

In 1792, Percy Bysshe Shelley was born at Field Place, an isolated country house set on a working farm in Sussex. As a child, Shelley's imagination took him to places that few children would venture. James Bieri, in his thoroughly documented biography *Percy Bysshe Shelley: A Biography*, wrote:

> One imaginary occupant of Field Place who found an important place in Bysshe's psyche was 'an Alchemist, old and grey, with a long beard.' The young explorer found a spacious garret under the roof where a lifted floorboard gave access to a deserted room where the alchemist lived.[10]

FIELD PLACE, BIRTHPLACE OF PERCY BYSSHE SHELLEY

This description was supported by Percy Bysshe Shelley's sister Helen, who remarked, "We were to go see him [the Alchemist] 'some day'; but we were content to wait and a cave was to be dug in the orchard for the better accommodation of this Cornelius Agrippa."[11] Note that Helen's choice of an alchemist most associated in her mind to childhood memories of her brother was Cornelius Agrippa, the same influential alchemist whose sudden appearance changes the life of the young Victor Frankenstein:

> When I was thirteen years of age, we all went on a party of pleasure to the baths near Thonon: the inclemency of the weather obliged us to remain a day confined to the inn. In this house I chanced to find a volume of the words of Cornelius Agrippa. I opened it with apathy; the theory which he attempts to demonstrate, and the wonderful facts which he relates, soon changed this feeling into enthusiasm. A new light seemed to dawn upon my mind. [12]

But this is not the end of Victor Frankenstein's study of alchemy. Frankenstein's personal engagement with this pre-scientific discipline is not a mere footnote to the novel but a rather critical theme that underlies the story:

> When I returned home, my first care was to procure the whole works of this author [Agrippa], and afterwards of Paracelsus and Albertus Magnus. I read and studied the wild fancies of these writers with delight; they appeared to me treasures known to few beside myself.[13]

And when Victor determined that he must share his new learning, a study which by most accounts was dangerously associated with man defying God's laws of nature, creation, and the sanctity of life, he discovered that those nearest him did not share in his enthusiasm. Fairly stated, his relationship to those nearest him were strained:

> And although I often wished to communicate these secret stores of knowledge to my father, yet his definite censure of my favorite Agrippa always withheld me. I disclosed my discoveries to Elizabeth, therefore, under a promise of strict secrecy; but she did not interest herself in the subject and I was left by her to pursue my studies alone.[14]

This alchemy-themed passage deserves special attention, for within it the very soul, mind, and dark memories of its author, Percy Bysshe Shelley, are evident.

Observe that it was the study of alchemy, the practice of which, on the one hand, was exploited by the Church for financial gain and yet also at the same time explicitly condemned by the Church[15], that marks a relational distance between Frankenstein and those nearest him. The relationship between alchemy and an implicit atheism among those who practiced it is crucial to mark. The Church condemned the practitioners of alchemy for their dabbling in matters best left to the Church alone, namely promising eternal life and transmuting one substance or essence into another. Only an atheist or heretic would dare to engage in a condemned study or practice, and worse yet Victor Frankenstein dares to share his findings with those around him.

That Victor would disgrace and dishonor his family by straying from the proper social path and deviating from the orthodox standards of religious faith shows much of Percy Shelley in Victor's character. Note well that it is in Victor's anti-Christian pursuit of learning that the first evidence of isolation between him and his father occurs. The dark and forbidden study of alchemy would also become a point of emotional distance between Victor Frankenstein and his would-be wife

Elizabeth. This autobiographical revelation is worth consideration, as it was while Percy Shelley was attending Oxford University that his relationship with his father, Timothy Shelley, was broken on account of a pamphlet written anonymously by Percy Shelley and his friend Thomas Jefferson Hogg—a pamphlet titled *The Necessity of Atheism*.

Timothy's reaction to his son's newfound conviction was less than encouraging:

> Timothy was angered and shamed by his son's public and provocative display of socially unacceptable ideas. Shelley had exposed his father's duplicitous religious stance, that private beliefs must not become public if they offend.[16]

Enraged by his son's behavior, Timothy appointed a "gentleman" to put Percy back on the proper path with the threat that if his son does not abandon his "errors" and "wicked opinions" the result would be to forfeit his relationship with his father and suffer "punishment and misery for the diabolical and wicked opinions."[17] Could Victor's fear of his father's disapproval for studying alchemy have been influenced by the paternal rejection that Percy suffered after publishing his anti-Christian ideas? The answer is self-apparent. It was not Mary Shelley who felt or experienced her father's rejection for pursuing or publishing ideas which were expressly forbidden by the Church, and it was not Mary who drew down such an experience and penned it into the story of Victor Frankenstein.

And what, if any, parallels link Victor Frankenstein's isolation from Elizabeth to Percy Bysshe Shelley? In Victor's case, the confession of his new passion for alchemy was met by his cousin and future wife Elizabeth with disinterest, and led to a solitary pursuit of alchemy; in short, it meant isolation as a consequence for sharing his inner secret knowledge. For Percy Bysshe Shelley, a corresponding experience with that of Victor Frankenstein arises on the occasion when Shelley shares his unorthodox ideas with his would-be wife and cousin, Harriet Grove. The similarities are uncanny and prove the event to be a defining moment in Shelley's life:

During the years 1809 and 1810 Shelley was not thinking more of his school friendships, studies and dilemmas than of his cousin Harriet Grove. It was felt in the family that he might marry this fresh and pretty girl, to whom (in the words of her brother) he "was at that time more attached than I can express."... Why then did nothing come of such hopes? ... Charles Grove mentions that after the holiday in London, when Shelley and Harriet had resumed their constant correspondence, "she became uneasy at the tone of his letters of speculative subjects.[18]

Observe:

(1) Both Victor and Percy are to be engaged to their cousins.

(2) Both Victor and Percy felt a sense of security and desire to disclose their newly discovered secret knowledge with their anticipated lifetime companions.

(3) For both Victor and Percy, the cost they paid for revealing their passion in such "speculative subjects" was that both men were left in a state of isolation and abandonment, whether physical or emotional.

Neither Victor nor Percy would ever find a true female companion to fully appreciate or understand their inner thoughts and intellectual pursuits. Percy immediately memorialized his feelings of hurt, anger, and betrayal over this first love lost in a poem included in an anonymously written book titled *Original Poetry by Victor and Cazire*.

Writing of Harriet's abandonment, Shelley declares:

Cold, cold is the blast when December is howling,
Cold are the damps on a dying Man's brow, —
Stern are the seas when the wild waves are rolling,
And sad is the grave where a loved one lies low;
But colder is scorn from the being who loved thee,
More stern is the sneer from the friend who has proved
thee,

More sad are the tears when their sorrows have moved
thee, Which mixed with groans anguish and wild
Madness Flow —

As already observed, Shelley also memorialized within the pages of *Frankenstein* the consequence of sharing his secret knowledge with the one he intended to marry. A simple substitution of names, Elizabeth for Harriet, maintaining the family relation as cousin, and the autobiography is seamless.

And still there is yet another gem hidden within this alchemical passage of *Frankenstein* which has already yielded a plethora of Victor and Percy associations; it is in Shelley's choice of words. Let us consider the passage another time from another angle:

And although I often wished to communicate *these secret stores of knowledge* to my father, yet his definite censure of my favorite Agrippa always withheld me. I disclosed my discoveries to Elizabeth, therefore, under a promise of strict secrecy; but she did not interest herself in the subject and I was left by her to pursue my studies alone. [emphasis added][19]

Given that this *Frankenstein* passage is deeply autobiographical, and that Shelley more than most writers intertwined himself and his experiences into his writing, it is not coincidental that in composing *Laon and Cythna* or *The Revolt of Islam,* during 1817, Shelley would echo his feelings with virtually the same words:

And from that hour did I with earnest thought
Heap *knowledge* from forbidden mines of lore,
Yet nothing that my tyrants knew or taught
I cared to learn, but from that *secret store*
Wrought linked armour for my soul, before
It might walk for to war among mankind;
Thus power and hope were strengthened more and more
Within me, till there came upon my mind
A sense of loneliness, a thirst with which I pined.[20]

When one takes into consideration that *Laon and Cythna* was composed during the same period in which *Frankenstein* was being written and that Shelley is in a deeply reflective state of mind concerning his boyhood fascination with forbidden alchemical authors and the cost it brought about, namely loneliness and isolation, it stands all the more evident that recurring ideas such as "forbidden mines of lore" and "secret store" and "a sense of loneliness" would match Victor's desire to communicate "secret stores of knowledge" only to find that he was left by Elizabeth to "pursue [his] studies alone."

Victor, however, does not let his isolation or emotional abandonment drive him far from his pursuit of knowledge, nor does Shelley abandon his intellectual curiosity in alchemy. As James Bieri observed, "the consuming enthusiasm of the child alchemist of Field Place"[21] continued to manifest itself in Shelley's role-playing, fire-starting, costumes, and chemical experiments.

Carl Grabo asserts that Shelley

...read books on magic and alchemy ... presumably through his interest in alchemy he turned early to the no less marvelous possibilities of electricity and chemistry, sciences which at the beginning of the nineteenth century were revealing new worlds to the imaginative mind. He conducted electrical and chemical experiments at home and at Eton where they were forbidden.[22]

A SHOCKING EXPERIENCE

The gradual progression in study from alchemy to the effects of electricity follows a predictable path for a student such as Shelley, and he would make use of these experiences as well when constructing the character of Victor Frankenstein. The pattern is quite clear: what Victor Frankenstein learns and experiences during his tumultuous life must have *first* taken place in the short and tumultuous life of its author, Percy Bysshe Shelley.

Anne K. Mellor, a noted Mary Shelley scholar, feminist, and Frankenstein expert, acknowledges the link between Shelley's alchemy and education in scientific uses of electricity and lightning:

Reading Darwin and Davy encouraged Percy Shelley in scientific speculations that he had embarked upon much earlier, as a school boy at Dr. Greenlaw's Syon House Academy in 1802. Inspired by the famous lectures of Dr. Adam Walker, which he heard again at Eton, Shelley began ten years of experiments with Leyden jars, microscopes, magnifying glasses, and chemical mixtures. His more memorable experiments left holes in his clothes and carpets, attempted to cure his sister Elizabeth's chilblains with a galvanic battery, and electrified a family tomcat. Shelley early learned to think of electricity and the processes of chemical attraction and repulsion as modes of a single polarized force. Adam Walker even identified electricity as the spark of life itself.[23]

The association of alchemy, chemistry, and use of electricity for affecting change, whether it be growth, reanimation, or sexual energy, is revealed early in the life of Percy Shelley just as it was in that of Victor Frankenstein:

When I was about fifteen years old, we had retired to our house near Belrive, when we witnessed a most violent and terrible thunderstorm. It advanced from behind the mountains of Jura; and the thunder burst at once with frightful loudness from various quarters of the heavens. I remained, while the storm lasted, watching its progress with curiosity and delight. As I stood at the door, on a sudden I beheld a stream of fire issue from an old and beautiful oak, which stood about twenty yards from our house; and so soon as the dazzling light vanished, the oak had disappeared, and nothing remained but a blasted stump. When we had visited it the next morning, we found the tree shattered in a singular manner... the catastrophe of this tree excited my extreme astonishment; and I eagerly inquired of my father the nature and origin of thunder and lightning. He replied, "Electricity;" he constructed a small electrical machine, and exhibited a few experiments; he made also a kite, with a wire, and string, which drew down that fluid from the clouds.[24]

Electricity, a key theme, often appeared in Shelley's poetry in such phrases as "creative fire," and "liquid love," or symbolized as the ethereal *fluid* of creation. The joining of science to alchemy came as a natural development in Shelley's thinking, first as the alchemist-inspired child at Field Place and later as a Benjamin Franklin experimentalist who had been tutored and lectured to by the most cutting-edge scientists of his day at Syon House and then later at Eton. As noted in the quotation by Anne K. Mellor, Adam Walker was the first to inspire the young Shelley. an inspiration which would have a profound impact on the author of *Frankenstein*.

ADAM WALKER WITH HIS FAMILY

ADAM WALKER

Adam Walker (1731–1821) was an English inventor, writer, and popular science lecturer. Mainly self-taught, he attended fashionable lectures on experimental philosophy in Manchester and established his own school there in 1762. For publicity he inserted advertisements in local papers and wrote a book entitled *Syllabus of a Course on Natural Philosophy* (Kendal, 1766). His syllabus covered 'Astronomy, the use of Globes, Pneumatics, Electricity, Magnetism, Chemistry, Mechanics, Hydrostatics, Hydraulics, Engineering, Fortifications, and Optics.'[25] As a lecturer he traveled to Syon House, the middle-class boarding school where Percy Bysshe Shelley spent his first years away from home. Syon House was located in Islesworth, on the Great Western Road in Thames Valley, and there between the years 1802 and 1804 Shelley first heard Dr. Adam Walker. It was on account of Walker's lectures that Shelley, like Victor Frankenstein, grew from a young alchemist to an avid amateur chemist, natural philosopher, and scientific experimenter. Carl Grabo comments that it was at Syon House that

> the transition of his interest from the occult to the scientific is by way of this love for the marvelous, for the new sciences of chemistry and electricity promised greater marvels than alchemy, marvels much more authentic, more possible of immediate realization.[26]

Likewise, James Bieri notes that "the lectures at Syon House on science and astronomy by the itinerant Dr. Adam Walker left an indelible imprint on Shelley."[27] That imprint most likely included an exposure to Walker's belief that

> [electricity's] power of exciting muscular motion in apparently dead animals, as well of increasing the growth, invigorating the stamina, and reviving diseased vegetation proves its relationship or affinity to the *living principle*.[28]

At Syon House, Shelley was not only taught the principles of reanimating the dead through the use of electricity, but he was also able to furnish himself with the proper apparatus for conducting the experiments which would terrify family, friends, pets, and schoolmates. According to Richard Holmes, it was Adam Walker's assistant who sold Shelley—or helped him build—his more advanced forms of electrical generators.[29]

Ian Jackson's "Science as Spectacle," in Knellwolf and Goodall's scholarly work *Frankenstein's Science*, observes

By the end of the eighteenth century, some electrical performers and their theories of electricity had become closely associated with social and political radicalism, making their enthusiastic embrace of the seemingly limitless potential of electricity all the more alarming for conservative critics, and all the more inspiring for those, including Percy Shelley (who had been taught by Adam Walker [1731–1821], one of the major radical electrical performers).[30]

And as to be expected, in the face of the obvious relationship of education and experience linking Percy Shelley to the characters and plot within *Frankenstein*, Jackson still arrives at the all too common and erroneous conclusion that

indirectly, Mary Shelley's conception of the plot and key scientific character of the novel was affected by her husband's studies of the secrets of nature. Percy Shelley was not only fascinated by the task of discovering the prime spark or essence of life but he also demonstrated a taste for the most spectacular manifestations of natural philosophy. This penchant towards the sensational and spectacular, not surprisingly, also characterized Victor Frankenstein.[31]

Thus, once again Percy Bysshe Shelley's education, experiences, and memories inadvertently spilled over and became the inspiration for Mary Shelley's work. Shelley was quite the leaky vessel and Mary was the most fortunate sponge by all such accounts.

Shelley providentially continued his education and slow transformation from young alchemist to scientist under Walker even after Shelley left Syon House Academy for Eton in 1804. The itinerant Walker became a lecturer at Eton during Shelley's tenure there as well.

Undoubtedly the most important and often overlooked influence on the young Shelley during the adolescent period of his life away from home was Dr. James Lind.

DR. JAMES LIND.
THIS SILHOUETTE IS THE ONLY KNOWN LIKENESS OF LIND.[32]

JAMES LIND

James Lind's role in Shelley's life, as described in the previous chapter, is monumental and worth a second look as it pertains to Shelley as an alchemist-scientist. While Lind is not mentioned in Knellwolf and Goodall's otherwise thorough book *Frankenstein's Science*, Lind's role as a contributor to the characters and plot in *Frankenstein* cannot be so easily dismissed. It was Dr. Lind, even more so than Dr. Walker, who guided and molded Shelley into becoming and imagining all that *Frankenstein* as a novel would come to represent. If, as it is argued, *Frankenstein* reflects the life, education, and experiences of Percy Bysshe Shelley, it follows that the men who influenced him the most would also be reflected most in his novel. The role that James Lind occupies in the formation of Percy Shelley is best revealed in Shelley's own words:

> This man ... is exactly what an old man ought to be. Free, calm-spirited, full of benevolence, and even of youthful ardour; his eye seemed to burn with supernatural spirit beneath his brow, shaded by his venerable white locks; he was tall, vigorous, and healthy in his body; tempered, as it had ever been, by his amiable mind. I owe that man far, ah! Far more than I owe to my father; he loved me and I shall never forget our long talks where he breathed the spirit of the kindest tolerance and purest wisdom.[33]

James Lind (1736–1812) was a Fellow of the Royal Society, physician to the royal household, a philosopher, inventor, scientist, and pamphleteer. More importantly, Lind was a virtual alchemist himself whose passionate interest in pushing scientific limits earned him the description as a "latter-day Paracelsus."[34] James Bieri writes that Lind's

> apparatus-filled study—embodied Shelley's childhood fantasies of the attic alchemist of Field Place ... Lind's influence may have extended to introducing Shelley to—or encouraging further study of Plato, Pliny, Lucretius, **Paracelsus**, **Albertus Magnus**, and Condorcet.[35]

The mention of Paracelsus and Albertus Magnus in relationship to Lind's influence on Shelley marks a clear indication that Lind and *Frankenstein* are united further than most researchers have ventured to admit.

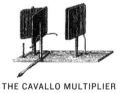

THE CAVALLO MULTIPLIER

As briefly noted in the previous chapter, The *Journal of the Royal Society of Medicine* in 2002 published an intriguing and insightful article by Christopher Goulding, M.Litt., titled "The Real Doctor Frankenstein." In the article, Mr. Goulding argues that in spite of recent Mary Shelley biographies which attempt to provide evidence of Mary's exposure to medical or scientific ideas, "... a reassessment of certain other medical themes and quasi-autobiographical events featured throughout *Frankenstein* might now be said to suggest the influence of Lind's character and work, via his pupil Percy Shelley." [36]

Goulding's methodical examination of the ties connecting Lind to *Frankenstein* is insightful and demands attention. Among the critical points of contact are Lind's contacts with Tiberio Cavallo (1749–1809), a noted Italian physicist and natural philosopher who invented the so-called Cavallo Multiplier, a device used for the amplification of small electric charges.

Between 1782 and 1809 Cavallo and Lind made a regular exchange of correspondence, in particular related to the question of Lind reanimating dead frogs. On July 11, 1792, Cavallo writes, "have you made any dead frogs jump like living ones," and on August 15 of the same year writes, "I am glad to hear of your success in the new experiments on muscular motion and earnestly entreat you to prosecute them to the *ne plus ultra* of possible means."[37] Further, Lind's medical training in Edinburgh with William Cullen (1710–1790), a Scottish physician, chemist, and professor at Edinburgh Medical School, reveals Lind's background in procedures for reviving a drowned or asphyxiated person. Cullen's work in this area was the established theory which was contained in Robert Thornton's *Medical Extracts*, a book which was ordered by Percy Shelley from his bookseller in 1812. The obvious relationship to *Frankenstein* is found in the revival of Victor Frankenstein when he is dragged, freezing and emaciated, aboard Walton's ship in the Arctic Ocean:

> We accordingly brought him back to the deck and restored him to animation by rubbing him with brandy, and forcing him to swallow a small quantity. As soon as he shewed signs of life, we wrapped him up in blankets, and placed him near the chimney of the kitchen-stove. By slow degrees he recovered, and ate a little soup, which restored him wonderfully.[38]

Understandably, Shelley was indebted to Lind for placing in his hands the medical background to conceive of using electricity to animate and reanimate animals, to revive those who had drowned or were near death from exposure to the elements, and also for bestowing on him the certainty that alchemical principles could be joined to modern scientific methods. To create, to heal, to resurrect; these possibilities were not so far separated from man and could be achieved without the aid of God and thereby effect a transformative change on mankind. Shelley's agenda, though deemed blasphemous to contemplate, would be unveiled for all to see in his writings and dangerous experiments.

Shelley's closest friend, Thomas Jefferson Hogg, provides a fitting and *shocking* illustration of how far Percy was willing to go with his childhood alchemical dreams joined to modern uses of electricity:

> He [Shelley] then proceeded, with much eagerness and enthusiasm, to show me the various instruments, especially the electrical apparatus; turning round the handle very rapidly, so that the fierce, crackling sparks flew forth; and presently standing upon the stool with glass feet, he begged me to work the machine until he was filled with the fluid, so that his long, wild locks bristled and stood on end. Afterwards he charged a powerful battery of several large jars; labouring with vast energy, and discoursing with increasing vehemence of the marvelous powers of electricity, of thunder and lightning; describing an electrical kite that he had made at home, and projecting another and an enormous one, or rather a combination of many kites, that would draw down from the sky an immense volume of electricity, the whole ammunition of a mighty thunderstorm; and this being directed to some point would there produce the most stupendous results.[39]

The question that the reader must ask again and again throughout this book is whether *Frankenstein* as originally penned anonymously in 1818 reflects the distinctive education and highly unusual personal experiences of Percy Bysshe Shelley (which he fictionalized into the novel and later credited to his wife in order to veil himself); *or* whether *Frankenstein* is a mere ghost story concocted in a waking dream by Mary Shelley, without the slightest "suggestion of one incident, nor scarcely of one train of feeling, to [her] husband." If the latter is true, Mary's gifts went far beyond writing; it must be admitted that her psychic abilities tapped so deeply into Shelley's past, without the slightest indication of his cooperation or awareness of it, that she virtually acted as a medium and channeled his memories and experiences. This indeed would be quite an accomplishment!

POSTSCRIPT

a selection from

ALASTOR: OR, THE SPIRIT OF SOLITUDE

December 14, 1815

I have made my bed in charnels and on coffins,
Where black death keeps record of the trophies won from
thee,
Hoping to still these obstinate questionings
Of Thee and thine, but forcing some lone ghost,
Thy messenger, to render up the tale of what we are.
In lone and silent hours,
When night makes a weird sound of its own stillness,
Like an inspired and desperate alchymist
Staking his very life on some dark hope,
Have I mixed awful talk and asking looks
With my most innocent love,
Until strange tears, uniting with those breathless kisses
made
Such magic as compels the charmed night
To render up thy charge ...

1 Mary Shelley, *Frankenstein, or the Modern Prometheus*, J. Paul Hunter, ed., *The Original 1818 Text Norton Critical Edition* (W.W. Norton and Co., 1996), p. 31

2 Ibid., (Preface, 1831) p. 172

3 Ibid., (Preface, 1831) p. 172

4 The 1932 MGM movie *Rasputin and the Empress* insinuated that the character Princess Natasha had been raped by Rasputin. Princess Natasha's character was supposedly intended to represent Princess Irina of Russia, and the real Princess Irina sued MGM for libel. After seeing the film twice, the jury agreed that the princess had been defamed.
Cf. en.wikipedia.org/wiki/All_persons_fictitious_disclaimer

5 Promotional photo of Boris Karloff from *The Bride of Frankenstein* as Frankenstein's monster: public domain image from commons.wikimedia.org/wiki/File:Frankenstein%27s_monster_(Boris_Karloff).jpg

6 Richard Holmes, *Shelley: The Pursuit* (E.P. Dutton & Co., Inc., 1975), p. 334

7 Ibid., p. 334

8 Mary Shelley, *Frankenstein, or the Modern Prometheus*, J. Paul Hunter, ed., *The Original 1818 Text Norton Critical Edition* (W.W. Norton and Co, 1996), p. 186

9 James Bieri, *Percy Bysshe Shelley: A Biography* (Johns Hopkins University Press, 2008) Preface, p. xi

10 Ibid., p. 37

11 Ibid., p. 37

12 Mary Shelley, *Frankenstein, or the Modern Prometheus*, J. Paul Hunter, ed., *The Original 1818 Text Norton Critical Edition* (W.W. Norton and Co., 1996), p. 21

13 Mary Shelley, *Frankenstein, or the Modern Prometheus*, J. Paul Hunter, ed., *The Original 1818 Text Norton Critical Edition* (W.W. Norton and Co., 1996), p. 22

14 Mary Shelley, *Frankenstein, or the Modern Prometheus*, J. Paul Hunter, ed., *The Original 1818 Text Norton Critical Edition* (W.W. Norton and Co., 1996), p. 22

15 In 1317 Pope John XXII issued a decree against the alchemists De Crimine Falsi Titulus VI. I Joannis XXII.

16 Bieri, p. 128

17 Ibid., p. 129

18 Edmund Blunden, *Shelley, A Life Story* (The Viking Press, 1947), pp. 45–46

19 Mary Shelley, *Frankenstein, or the Modern Prometheus*, J. Paul Hunter, ed., *The Original 1818 Text Norton Critical Edition* (W.W. Norton and Co., 1996), p. 22

20 Donald H. Reiman and Neil Fraistat, eds., *Shelley's Poetry and Prose* (W.W. Norton & Co., 2002), p. 102

21 Bieri, p. 37

22 Carl Grabo, *Shelley's Eccentricities* (University of New Mexico Press, 1950), pp. 8–9

23 Anne K. Mellor, *A Feminist Critique of Science,* homepage.ntlworld.com/chris.thorns/resources/Franken-stein/A_Feminist_Critique_of_Science.pdf

24 Mary Shelley, *Frankenstein, or the Modern Prometheus*, J. Paul Hunter, ed., *The Original 1818 Text Norton Critical Edition* (W.W. Norton and Co., 1996), pp. 22–23

25 cf. en.wikipedia.org/wiki/Adam_Walker_(inventor)

26 Carl Grabo, *A Newton Among Poets* (University of North Carolina Press, 1930), p. 4

27 Bieri, p. 50

28 Adam Walker, *System of Familiar Philosophy*: *In Twelve Lectures* (London, 1799), p. 391; original emphasis is retained.

29 Holmes, p. 16

30 Ian Jackson, contributor, Christian Knellwolf and Jane Goodall, editors, *Frankenstein's Science: Experimentation and Discovery in Romantic Culture, 1780–1830* (Ashgate, 2008), p. 152.

31 Ibid., p. 152

32 Image of Lind found at www.jameslind.co.uk, a website maintained by Christopher Goulding

33 Thomas Jefferson Hogg, *The Life of Percy Bysshe Shelley,* 2 volumes. 1858. Op cit. Richard Holmes, *Shelley: The Pursuit,* p. 28

34 Bieri, p. 65

35 Ibid, pp. 65–66 (emphasis added to original quotation)

36 Christopher Goulding, "The Real Doctor Frankenstein?" published in the *Journal of the Royal Society of Medicine*, 2002 May; 95(5): 257–259. Online article: www.ncbi.nlm.nih.gov/pmc/articles/PMC1279684

37 Ibid.

38 Mary Shelley, *Frankenstein, or the Modern Prometheus*, J. Paul Hunter, ed., *The Original 1818 Text Norton Critical Edition* (W.W. Norton and Co., 1996), p. 14

39 Holmes, pp. 44–45

CHAPTER 3

PERCY SHELLEY, FRANKENSTEIN, AND ATHEISM

Oh how I wish I were the Antichrist.[1]
— Percy Bysshe Shelley

The story of *Frankenstein* is a subtle, albeit powerful, manifesto for atheism in the hands of Percy Shelley. At first glance such a claim may seem far-fetched, perhaps forced; however, a careful reading of *Frankenstein* reveals that Shelley had every intention to espouse his conviction regarding the dangers of religion, specifically the Christian faith. From an early age Shelley determined that he would expose and covertly attack the Church as an instrument of terror, injustice, and hypocrisy. *Frankenstein* stands as his most cleverly concealed literary attempt to effect an awakening by undermining credibility in the Christian faith. Shelley vowed,

> Oh! I burn with impatience for the moment of Xtianity's [sic] dissolution, it has injured me; I swear on the altar of perjured love to revenge myself on the hated cause of the effect which even now I can scarcely help deploring — Indeed I think it is to the benefit of society to destroy the opinions which can annihilate the dearest of its ties ... *I will stab the wretch in secret.* Let us hope that the wound which we inflict tho' the dagger be concealed, will rankle in the heart of our adversary.[2]

Although these words do not make any explicit reference to the writing of *Frankenstein*, they do in fact reveal his ultimate goal as an author: to secretly destroy Christianity and drive a fatal dagger into it by means of his writings. Assuming Percy Shelley to be the author of *Frankenstein*, the novel *ought to* reveal something of Shelley's atheistic vow in the previous cited quotation.

AN ATHEIST AND AN ANGLICAN PRIEST

Shelley's revolutionary and atheistic agenda openly manifested itself shortly after he began his studies at the University of Oxford in 1810. Determined to rid the world of tyranny, Shelley could identify no greater target deemed more oppressive to human freedom than the Christian religion. Shelley began a calculated and systematic plan to bait Anglican clerics into discussions with him by mailing seemingly innocent letters to his chosen ecclesiastical pawns. These letters, if replied to, would provide Shelley with a theological and intellectual punching bag upon which to try out his arguments.. This research into Christian apologetics prepared the ground for much of the atheistic works which would soon follow. Shelley wanted first-hand evidence as to how England's best clergymen and theologians would respond to ostensibly sincere requests for answers from a person struggling to believe the Christian faith. The responses to his pseudonymously written letters to the clergymen enabled Shelley to align his intellectual crosshairs squarely on his religious targets; the end result of Shelley's cat-and-mouse game was his tract *The Necessity of Atheism*, anonymously published in 1811.

It is curious that *The Necessity of Atheism* is less atheistic than it is a challenge to theists to acknowledge that *belief* is a human *passion*, and as such cannot stand up to the test of being *reasonable*, thus the necessity or reasonableness of atheism. Atheism, in Shelley's case, is an argument for human reason to be given preeminence over passions, which are always subjective, lacking reasonable proof, and therefore can not be enforced upon any free person. Newman Ivey White summarizes Shelley's tract accurately, writing

Except for the title and the signature to the advertisement ("through deficiency of proof, an Atheist.") there was no atheism in it. In its seven pages of text it argued that belief can come only from three sources: physical experience, reason based on experience, and the experience of others, or testimony. None of these, it argued, establishes the existence of a deity, and belief, which is not subject to the will, is impossible until they do. Hence the existence of a God is not proved.[3]

Shelley's words were temperate, reasoned, and yet also revolutionary at the beginning of the nineteenth century, a century still reeling from the effects of the American War for Independence and the French Revolution:

The mind cannot believe the existence of a creative God: it is also evident that, as belief is a passion of the mind, no degree of criminality is attachable to disbelief; and that they only are reprehensible who neglect to remove the false medium through which their mind views any subject of discussion. Every reflecting mind must acknowledge that there is no proof of the existence of a Deity.[4]

It did not take long before Percy Bysshe Shelley was found out and brought before the Master of University College, Oxford, Rev. James Griffith. Shelley was questioned amidst much anger from the Master of the college concerning his part in writing the anonymous atheistic tract. Shelley's response to Griffith was,

If I can judge from your manner ... you are resolved to punish me, if I should acknowledge that it is my work. If you can prove that it is, produce your evidence; it is neither just nor lawful to interrogate me in such a case and for such a purpose. Such proceedings would become a court of inquisitors, but not free men in a free country.[lxxxiii]

And with his patriotic appeal for evidence to be produced, Percy Bysshe Shelley was expelled from the University of Oxford. Before the University gates could slam behind him, Shelley had already sent the tract on atheism to all of the bishops, and apparently to many professors, heads of colleges, the Vice Chancellor, and at least one Cambridge professor.[6] Ironically, in the grand tradition of sanctifying sinners into saints—if such men or women achieve fame after their deaths—a monument now resides at University College, Oxford, to pay homage to the University's most famous expelled atheist.

For Shelley, however, still being quite alive in 1811 and not so saintly as death would later make him, this event only tempered his steel and focused his aim for future literary projects. He learned from this event that greater care must be taken to remain anonymous, to conceal his agenda, and to mislead those who were most likely to assume his part in such future affairs. Writing to his co-la-

PERCY BYSSHE SHELLEY MEMORIAL, UNIVERSITY COLLEGE, OXFORD

borer in the infamous *Necessity of Atheism* tract, Thomas Jefferson Hogg, Shelley revealed his new design, a plan in which Shelley would suggest to the public that he had given up writing:

> ...I give out therefore that I will publish no more; every one here, but the select few who enter into its schemes believed my assertion. [7]

Of course nothing was further from his mind than to abandon his vow to thrust his dagger deeply into the heart of the Christian faith. From this point forward Shelley would guard his "schemes" among the select few who could be trusted and he would learn even better how to apply the principles of a quiet revolution. He reasserted his vow to Hogg, exclaiming, "yet here I swear and if I break my oath may Infinity Eternity blast me, here I swear that never will I forgive Christianity."[8]

AN ATHEIST QUEEN (MAB)

Within a year Shelley struck again in a privately distributed, though initially unpublished, poem titled *Queen Mab*. Whereas *The Necessity of Atheism* relied on a reasoned and logical appeal to the reader, *Queen Mab* took aim at the heart. Speaking in the voice of God, a powerful literary device calculated to shock his selected reader into dread or into an alarmed state of reasonable doubt concerning the schizophrenic nature of the God of Holy Scripture, Shelley [or God, if you dare] declares:

> From an eternity of idleness
> I, God, awoke; in seven days' toil made earth
> From nothing; rested, and created man:
> I placed him in a paradise, and there
> Planted the tree of evil, so that he
> Might eat and perish, and my soul procure
> Wherewith to sate its malice, and to turn,
> Even like a heartless conqueror of the earth,
> All misery to my fame. The race of men
> Chosen to my honor, with impunity
> May sate the lusts I planted in their heart.
> Here I command thee hence to lead them on,
> Until, with hardened feet, their conquering troops
> Wade on the promised soil through woman's blood.
> And make my name be dreaded through the land.
> Yet ever-burning flame and ceaseless woe
> Shall be the doom of their eternal souls,
> With every soul on this ungrateful earth,
> Virtuous or vicious, weak or strong, — even all
> Shall perish, to fulfil [sic] the blind revenge
> (which you, to men, call justice) of their God.[9]

And to drive the dagger of atheism in deeper, Shelley added the following advice in his notes accompanying the poem:

Religion and morality, as they now stand, compose a practical code of misery and servitude: the genius of human happiness must tear every leaf from the accursed book of God ere man can read the inscription on his heart.[10]

By 1813 Shelley had arrived at the conclusion that "reason" is inherent to human nature, it is objectively verifiable, and resonates within the fiber of each living person, and therefore the most capable means of moving the senses and will to act. Logic paired with a strong emotional appeal was well suited for his poetry, and this was precisely the purpose and effect of *Queen Mab*.

PRE-*FRANKENSTEIN* ATHEISTIC AND ALCHEMISTIC FICTION

And it was not only atheistic poetry that Shelley made use of at this time; he also put his hand to writing godless fiction. His short novels *Zastrozzi* (1810) and *St. Irvyne, or the Rosicrucian* (1811), though largely unnoticed by the public—aside from a few condemning reviews[11]—proved suitable mediums for testing his hand at infusing atheistic and alchemistic themes into fiction. In these first works of fiction Shelley developed characters, settings, and plots which would reappear in a more advanced form only a few years later during a stormy summer in Geneva.

A cursory overview of *St. Irvyne* (1811) bears an uncanny similarity to *Frankenstein*. Consider a few overlapping points of interest: a solitary wanderer through the Alps; characters settled in Geneva; a mysterious dark figure who is always nearby and yet elusive; deceptions which lead to murder; and an alchemist whose studies lead him to the discovery of eternal life. This cannot be coincidental!

Shelley's earliest atheistic and alchemistic fiction demonstrates *Frankenstein* was not birthed in the context of a young girl's waking dream, it was a seed germinating in Shelley's mind and leaking from his quill for many years; more importantly, it was the story of his own life and convictions. Shelley's final novel, *Frankenstein*, a far more advanced alchemistic and atheistic work, would be his unacknowledged crowning achievement, for in this novel he could fictionalize all of his mature experiences, education, and atheistic propaganda in a single *opus*.

PROMETHEUS AND STEALING GOD'S FIRE: SHELLEY'S ATHEISM TAKES SHAPE

The subtitle to *Frankenstein* is the first indication that the novel is intended as a challenge to the Christian god. *The Modern Prometheus* harkens the reader of *Frankenstein* to a remembrance of the Greek titan Prometheus, who was chained and tortured for stealing fire from Zeus in order to give light to humanity as well as for his thwarting of Zeus' plan to annihilate the human race. One can hardly mistake the *modus operandi* of Percy Shelley even in the subtitle of *Frankenstein*. Who more clearly could identify with the rebellious Prometheus than Shelley, who had been stealing God's fire since his days at Oxford?

As early as 1810, when Shelley matriculated to the University of Oxford, he was engaged in the reading of Aeschylus' *Prometheus Bound,* and mere months before undertaking *Frankenstein* during the stormy summer of 1816 Shelley was once again reading as well as translating Aeschylus' Greek version of *Prometheus Bound*. Shelley's initial interest, timed conveniently to his writing of *The Necessity of Atheism*, as well as his return to the Prometheus myth in its original language—alongside the writing of *Frankenstein, or the Modern Prometheus*—suggests more than coincidence. Equally noteworthy is the fact that Shelley's attachment to this atheistic and revolutionary theme carried over *after* the completion of *Frankenstein* in 1818 when he began his four-act play *Prometheus Unbound* in October of the same year.

The atheism and social revolution that Shelley subtly embedded in *Frankenstein, or The Modern Prometheus* plot would reappear in his far less subtle four-act play *Prometheus Unbound*, a virtual commentary behind the ideas veiled in his novel. In his Preface to *Prometheus Unbound,* Shelley again acknowledges his underlying purpose as an author, a purpose as true for his four-act play as it is for his 1818 novel *Frankenstein*:

Poets, not otherwise than philosophers, painters, sculptors, and musicians, are in one sense the creators and in another the creations of their age... let this opportunity be conceded to me of acknowledging that I have, what a Scotch philosopher characteristically terms, 'a passion for reforming the world.'[12]

Shelley saw his literary purpose as that of a creator and reformer, and therefore used the revolutionary Promethean theme of a lesser being challenging the authority of God to enlighten and save the human race. What *is* surprising is that so few scholars have taken Shelley at his word and acknowledged that his life and literary purpose was to effect a reformation and create a new, alchemically inspired society without the need of God. What could be more fitting to style his literary agenda upon than Prometheus' defiance of Zeus?

A DIGRESSION: SHELLEY'S WORDS, MARY'S HAND

An incalculably important, though seemingly tangential, detail as it relates to the procedure Shelley used in writing for publication was his habit of employing Mary in the transcribing process. The final *Frankenstein* transcripts sent to press were penned in Mary Shelley's hand and for this reason are generally promoted as a final nail-in-the-coffin argument for Mary's authorship of the novel. Yet as Reiman and Fraistat acknowledge in *Shelley's Poetry and Prose*,

Mary Shelley transcribed for the press most or all of Acts I–III [*Prometheus Unbound*] between September 5 and 12, 1819, and all of Act IV in mid-December 1819. *As was his usual practice*, Shelley appears to have corrected the press transcripts, making a series of small final revisions to prepare the poem for the press.[13]

There is no logical rationale for assuming that *Frankenstein, or the Modern Prometheus* was written and transcribed in any other fashion than that which Reiman and Fraistat admit was Shelley's "usual practice," namely Shelley created and wrote his first drafts (or on occasion dictated them[14]) while Mary took on the role as his final transcriber. Curiously, this well-known practice of Shelley's continues to be intentionally overlooked by *Frankenstein* scholars who merely count the few thousand words that Shelley *corrected* in the *Frankenstein* press transcript.

In 2008 Charles E. Robinson applied this defective method of ignoring Shelley's "usual practice" when he graciously credited Percy Bysshe Shelley with a minimal 4,000- to 5,000-word contribution to *Frankenstein*.[15] Why, one may ask, is it "his usual practice" when Shelley makes "small final revisions" to *Prometheus Unbound*—as well as many other works—and then remarkably it is no longer Shelley's "*usual* practice" when his hand makes minimal corrections to *Frankenstein, or The Modern Prometheus*? The reader would do well to pay diligent attention to this point while reassessing the evidence behind the 1818 anonymously published first edition of *Frankenstein*.

The fact that *Frankenstein* became shrouded beneath the thinly fabricated veil of Mary's authorship greatly assisted Shelley's intention to attack his victim, Christianity, without notice. It is the primary thesis of this book that the fundamental reason Percy Bysshe Shelley perpetrated the hoax of Mary Shelley as *Frankenstein*'s author was his calculated agenda to initiate his alchemical and atheistic social revolution without suspicion or detraction from the novel by association with his name and atheistic reputation. Had the name of England's most notorious atheist been attached to *Frankenstein*, his anti-Christian revolutionary agenda would have been far more obvious and consequently far less effective. A terrorist's or revolutionary's most powerful weapon is in the ability to remain anonymous and unpredictable. For Percy Bysshe Shelley, his war was one without guns or knives but with a sharp wit and a quill, yet all the same it was a personal engagement against an enemy: against those he considered agents of tyranny, in particular the Church, and his success demanded that he be covert in his operations.

THE HIDDEN ATHEISM IN *FRANKENSTEIN*

The question now must be asked, how did Shelley covertly weave his atheistic agenda into the literary fabric of *Frankenstein*? In two subtle though identifiable ways: the first and more easily observed one was to create a plot in which a single man achieves the high and blasphemous act of creating life without the participation of God. Victor Frankenstein accomplishes through his childhood study of alchemy and his university education in modern science a feat which only God could have been capable of achieving—the grand gift of giving life. Note, it is the spark of electricity rather than the breath of the Holy Spirit which bestowed life. Nature in effect supplanted God and, consequently, man's ability to harness nature's power was, in effect, to enthrone man at the highest position in all of creation. The threat of an angry god could no longer be used to tyrannize and force mankind into submission. A knowledge of nature with all of its beauty and possibilities would, if scientifically applied, naturally liberate mankind from the domination of priests, bishops, and the governments which acted in collusion with the Church. *Frankenstein* was the catalyst for revolution if only Shelley's readers could read between the lines.

One might argue that if this was Shelley's intended agenda, why would the novel end in Victor Frankenstein's apparent failure? Is this not counterproductive to Shelley's purpose? Quite the opposite is true. Shelley cleverly answers this anticipated dilemma in his own *review* of the work that he authored:

> In this the direct moral of the book consists; and it is perhaps the most important, and of the most universal application, of any moral that can be enforced by example. Treat a person ill, and he will become wicked. Requite affection with scorn; — let one being be selected, for whatever cause, as the refuse of his kind — divide him, a social being, from society, and you impose upon him the irresistible obligations — malevolence and selfishness. It is thus that, too often in society, those who are best qualified to be its benefactors and its ornaments, are branded by some accident with scorn, and changed, by neglect and solitude of heart, into a scourge and a curse.[16]

One can hardly miss the autobiographical content in Shelley's review of *Frankenstein*. He had experienced beatings and bullying while at Syon Academy and Eton on account of his feminine or androgynous demeanor and appearance; been labeled "mad" and "dangerous" by his peers and those in authority over him during his adolescence; was ostracized by his sisters, threatened with disinheritance by his father; expelled from the University of Oxford; attacked by the press for his radical ideas and writings; and lived most of his short life misunderstood by those around him. Shelley was the very image of the fiend, the creature, the unwanted "refuse of his kind" who might have been a benefactor to mankind but instead became its curse. The message and moral is quite clear: Frankenstein's creature was not the failure, but rather, society's inability to live in harmony with nature while submitting to the irrational authority of a divinity was the primary cause of evil, the actual failure. Society under the dominating authority of religion is what is truly monstrous. For Shelley, God's being, laws, and threats are unnecessary for the establishing of morality in mankind; there is no need to blame "the devil" for society's ills. The fault lies squarely on society for its refusal to act in accordance with nature and with respect to its inherent goodness. The creature in *Frankenstein* bears responsibility for his actions but one must concede that, had the "fiend" been treated in accordance with the love that was due to it at the moment of its self-awareness, the creature of Victor Frankenstein would have understood, experienced, and reciprocated goodness rather than evil. Shelley's moral philosophy was expressed poetically in *Peter Bell the Third*:

> The Devil, I safely can aver,
> Has neither hoof, nor tail, nor sting;
> Nor is he, as some sages swear,
> A spirit, neither here nor there,
> In nothing—yet in everything.
> He is—what we are;[17]

The second manner in which *Frankenstein* thrusts Shelley's atheistic dagger at the heart of Christianity occurs when Justine, the Frankenstein household's servant, is falsely accused of the murder of young William, Victor's brother. Only days after making a case for herself in court, arguing that she had been framed and evidence had been planted on her by the actual murderer—whoever he/she/it was—Justine makes a sudden and inexplicable reversal. Much to the horror of the Frankenstein family, Justine confesses to the murder when in fact she is innocent. After Justine is pressed by Victor and his sister-like cousin and future wife Elizabeth to explain why she has now reversed herself and confessed to the murder, Justine declares,

> I did confess; but I confessed a lie. I confessed, that I might obtain absolution; but now that falsehood lies heavier at my heart than all my other sins. The God of heaven forgive me! Ever since I was condemned, my confessor has besieged me; he threatened and menaced, until I almost began to think that I was the monster that he said I was. He threatened excommunication and hell fire in my last moments, if I continued obdurate... In an evil hour I subscribed to a lie; and now only am I truly miserable.[18]

In a clever and unsuspecting manner, Shelley finds a way to bypass and undermine the strongest defense mechanism of the faithful: that implicit trust which refuses to believe the Church could err; the Church is, after all, the earthly voice and tribunal for God. The reader, now sympathizing with Justine, has been compelled to see reality from a new perspective and thereby feels repulsion toward the Church and empathy for a poor servant. Justine, as a Shelleyan analogy for all of the oppressed servants of a false god, does the unthinkable and betrays her own conscience in hopes of escaping excommunication and hellfire. The moral dilemma is apparent, and the human heart responds; the mind of each reader is engaged to ask, why would the Church or a benevolent god exercise such emotional torture against his own creation? What are the consequences of betraying one's own conscience? In this well-contrived episode

Shelley introduces his own parable with Justine as the sheep led to the slaughter by clergy acting in the capacity of God's messengers of doom. The effect is an emotional shock and an awakening of human reason as Shelley planned it. The reader is compelled to do the unthinkable—to judge the moral authority of the Church on account of its egregious crime against Justine. In the priest's coercing of this innocent servant to confess to a crime which she did not commit, the Church is exposed for its abuse and tyranny over the innocent with its threat of eternal punishment. Utilizing its authority to speak with the voice of God, Shelley anticipates that the reader will awaken to see the Church as an unnecessary and inhumane tyrannous institution perpetually inflicting torture on humanity, while furthering its own self-appointed and incontestable position to remain the moral referees holding the power to grant eternal life or threaten eternal punishment; the keys of Saint Peter, to bind or to loose on earth as in heaven. Shelley, the atheist, accomplished his purpose with hardly being noticed. The story might well have been written with Justine being framed and executed for a crime committed by the fiend without the need to introduce this twist of a false confession. However, by inserting this twist and turning the reader against the Church, opening the eyes of the readers to question the moral authority of the Church, Shelley has hit his mark and the dagger is lodged deeply into the heart of his truest enemy, the Christian church.

The fiend murdered young William in his rage against his maker, but how does one explain the Church standing equally guilty for the execution (murder) of innocent Justine? In Shelley's subtle way, the fiend elicits the reader's sympathy, or at least understanding, while the Church finds no sympathy whatsoever and becomes the greater monster in the novel.

In one additional atheistic-tilting episode described in Volume 2, chapter 7, the cottagers' (De Lacey, Felix, Agatha, and Safie) sad history is revealed to Frankenstein's creature. In an act of sincere human compassion, Felix risks his own life to deliver (jail break) a Turk who has been unjustly sentenced to death for no greater reason than his unpopular religion or *false* god. The Turk, promising his daughter (Safie) to his deliverer (Felix), takes the first opportunity of his newly found freedom to betray his promise and withdraw Safie from Felix! The reason for the betrayal and broken engagement of the lovers? The Turk could not bear to think of his Muslim daughter married to a non-Muslim, even if it was the same man who delivered him. Thus, Felix's humanitarian act, inspired by compassion and without any regard for religion or the god behind it, was rewarded with evil by the one who believed in God and allowed his religion to divide, betray, and hurt the good, innocent, and those who were revealed as "society's benefactors." In Shelley's hands, the creature learns that those who trust in God cannot be trusted in human relationships! Atheism's agenda once again is subtly inserted to draw the reader away from faith and is thrown toward human reason, unaided by the need of a god or Holy Spirit.

SHELLEY ENCOUNTERS THE DEVIL

And now to reveal one of the most curious events linking the life of Percy Bysshe Shelley to the characters and events in *Frankenstein*, Shelley's encounter with the devil himself! It occurred under circumstances not entirely unique for a meeting with a devil or fiend; it began on Friday, 26 February 1813. The night was dark and stormy with gale-force winds blowing in from Caernarvon Bay. Percy and his first wife Harriet were renting a home in Tan-yr-Allt, northern Wales, and for some unexplained reason that evening Percy went upstairs to bed prepared with two loaded pistols. The rest of the story is best related by Harriet in a letter written to Thomas Hookham, 12 March 1813:

> Mr. S. [Shelley] promised you a recital of the horrible events that caused us to leave Wales. I have undertaken the task, as I wish to spare him, in the present nervous state of his health, every thing that can recal [sic] to his mind the horrors of that night, which I will relate. On Friday night, the 26th February, we retired to bed between ten and eleven o'clock. We had been in bed about half an hour, when Mr. S. heard a noise proceeding from one of the par-

lours. He immediately went down stairs with two pistols, which he had loaded that night, expecting to have occasion for them. He went into the billiard room, where he heard footsteps retreating. He followed into another little room, which was called an office. He there saw a man in the act of quitting the room through a glass window which opens into the shrubbery. The man fired at Mr. S., which he avoided. Bysshe then fired, but it flashed in the pan. The man then knocked Bysshe down, and they struggled on the ground. Bysshe then fired his second pistol, which he thought wounded him in the shoulder, as he uttered a shriek and got up, when he said these words: *By God. I will be revenged! I will murder your wife. I will ravish your sister. By God I will be revenged.* He then fled—as we hoped for the night. Our servants were not gone to bed, but were just going, when this horrible affair happened. This was about eleven o'clock. We all assembled in the parlour, where we remained for two hours. Mr. S. then advised us to retire, thinking it impossible he would make a second attack. We left Bysshe and our manservant, who had only arrived that day, and who knew nothing of the house, to sit up. I had been in bed three hours when I heard a pistol go off. I immediately ran downstairs, when I perceived that Bysshe's flannel gown had been shot through, and the window curtain. Bysshe had sent Daniel to see what hour it was, when he heard a noise at the window. He went there, and a man thrust his arm through the glass and fired at him. Thank heaven! The ball went through his gown and he remained unhurt, Mr. S. happened to stand sideways; had he stood fronting, the ball must have killed him. Bysshe fired his pistol, but it would not go off. He then aimed a blow at him with an old sword which he found in the house. The assassin attempted to get the sword from him, and just as he was pulling it away Dan rushed the room, when he made his escape.[19]

The assassination attempt or break-in story takes a further twist with the account related the morning after the event to John Williams, Shelley's friend. According to Williams,

Shelley had seen a face against the window and had fired at it, shattering the glass. He had then rushed out upon the lawn, where he saw the devil leaning against a tree. As he told his story, Shelley seized pen and ink and sketched this vision upon a wooden screen and then attempted to burn the screen in order to destroy the apparition. The screen was saved with some difficulty, but was subsequently lost, not however before a copy of Shelley's sketch was made.

SHELLEY'S JEERING-FACED
TAN-YR-ALLT DEVIL

THE SECOND COMING OF THE TAN-YR-ALLT DEVIL

If the event sounds suspiciously familiar, consider the threatening words of Frankenstein's demonic creature on the occasion of it learning that Victor has destroyed its hopes for a mate:

Beware! Your hours will pass in dread and misery, and soon the bolt will fall which must ravish from you and your happiness for ever. Are you to be happy, while I grovel in the intensity of my wretchedness? You can blast my other passions; but revenge remains — revenge.[20]

And the moment of revenge as related by Victor Frankenstein:

> It was eight o'clock when we landed; we walked for a short time on the shore, enjoying the transitory light, and then retired to the inn, and contemplated the lovely scene of waters, woods, and mountains, obscured in darkness, yet still displaying their black outlines.
>
> The wind, which had fallen in the south, now rose with great violence in the west ... suddenly a heavy storm of rain descended. I had been calm during the day; but so soon as night obscured the shapes of objects, a thousand fears arose in my mind. I was anxious and watchful, while my right hand grasped a pistol which was hidden in my bosom; every sound terrified me; but I resolved that I would sell my life dearly, and not relax the impeding conflict until my own life, or that of my adversary, were extinguished...
>
> I happened to look up. The windows of the room had before been darkened; and I felt a kind of panic on seeing the pale yellow light of the moon illuminate the chamber. The shutters had been thrown back; and with a sensation of horror not to be described, I saw at the open window a figure the most hideous and abhorred. A grin was on the face of the monster; he seemed to jeer, as with his fiendish finger he pointed towards the corpse of my wife. I rushed towards the window, and drawing a pistol from my bosom, shot; but he eluded me.[21]

Is it *just* possible that the Tan-yr-Allt demon whose presence appeared suddenly at the window of a home in a remote region on a stormy evening, and then threatening vengeance against Shelley and promising to kill his wife, might have reappeared in Percy Bysshe Shelley's autobiographical novel *Frankenstein* under a similar jeering form? An elusive demon, vengeful and murderous, suddenly appearing at a window on a stormy night at an inn located in a remote region intent on murdering Victor Frankenstein's wife?

The similarities are surely monumental enough to convince even the most ardent of Mary Shelley defenders to blushingly confess that Mary undoubtedly must have—once again—taken Percy's memories and embedded them into her ghost story. Memories which were more than a little awkward considering the fact that it was not Mary who was nestled in with Percy at Tan-yr-Allt that evening; rather the event occurred with and was recorded by his first wife Harriet, who was abandoned by Percy after he met Mary.

The conspiracy theory may slowly begin to seem quite reasonable when placed against the growing evidence that the *Frankenstein* story was drawn from the memories, education, and experiences of Percy Bysshe Shelley, a man who simply conspired with his then-mistress, Mary Godwin, to hide his name and later attribute the authorship to her. The demon story is one more example of how the atheist Percy Bysshe Shelley came to write the 1818 first edition of *Frankenstein*.

1 Percy Bysshe Shelley, *The Letters of Percy Bysshe Shelley,* F.L. Jones, ed., (Oxford University Press, 1964), I. No. 35, p. 35

2 Richard Holmes, *Shelley: The Pursuit* (E.P. Dutton & Co., Inc., 1975), p. 46

3 Newman Ivey White, *Shelley* (2 Vol.) (Alfred A. Knopf, 1940), p. 113, vol. 1

4 Percy Bysshe Shelley, *The Necessity of Atheism*, first published anonymously in 1811 and revised in *Notes to Queen Mab* 1813; www.infidels.org/library/historical/percy_shelley/necessity_of_atheism.html

5 James Bieri, *Percy Bysshe Shelley: A Biography* (Johns Hopkins University Press, 2008), p. 124. *op. cit.*, Thomas Jefferson Hogg, *The Life of Percy Bysshe Shelley*, 2 volumes. (London, 1858)

6 Ibid., p. 122

7 Holmes, p. 46

8 Ibid., p. 47

9 Donald H. Reiman and Neil Fraistat, eds., *Shelley's Poetry and Prose*, (W.W. Norton & Co., 2002), pp. 56–57 www.english.upenn.edu/~curran/250/mabnotes.html

10 "Zastrozzi is one of the most savage and improbable demons that ever issued from a diseased brain." cf. en.wikipedia.org/wiki/Zastrozzi

11 Donald H. Reiman and Neil Fraistat, eds., *Shelley's Poetry and Prose*, (W.W. Norton & Co., 2002), p. 208

12 Ibid., p. 204

13 cf. *Journal of Edward Ellerker Williams*, with an introduction by Richard Garnett (1902), London, Elkin Mathews

14 Charles E. Robinson, ed., *Frankenstein, or The Modern Prometheus: The Original Two-Volume Novel of 1816–1817 from the Bodleian Library Manuscripts by Mary Wollstonecraft Shelley* (Vintage Books, 2008), p. 25

15 Mary Shelley, *Frankenstein, or the Modern Prometheus*, J. Paul Hunter, ed., *The Original 1818 Text Norton Critical Edition* (W.W. Norton & Co., 1996), p. 186. *Op. cit., On Frankenstein* by Percy Bysshe Shelley, written in 1817; published (posthumously) in *The Athenaeum Journal of Literature, Science and the Fine Arts,* Nov. 10, 1832

16 Percy Bysshe Shelley, *Peter Bell the Third* (Composed 1819; Published 1839 in Mary Shelley's 2nd Edition of *The Collected Works of Percy Bysshe Shelley*)

17 Mary Shelley, *Frankenstein, or the Modern Prometheus*, J. Paul Hunter, ed., *The Original 1818 Text Norton Critical Edition* (W.W. Norton & Co., 1996), p. 56

18 Richard Holmes, *Shelley: The Pursuit* (E.P. Dutton & Co., Inc., 1975), pp. 191–193

19 Newman Ivey White, *Shelley* (2 Vol.) (Alfred A. Knopf, 1940), p. 281, vol. 1

20 Mary Shelley, *Frankenstein, or the Modern Prometheus*, J. Paul Hunter, ed., *The Original 1818 Text Norton Critical Edition* (W.W. Norton & Co., 1996), p. 116

21 Ibid., p. 136

CHAPTER 4

SHELLEY: THE ANONYMOUS ILLUMINATIST

...I give out therefore that I will publish no more; every one here, but the select few who enter into its schemes believed my assertion.[1]

— Percy Bysshe Shelley

MISDIRECTION AND DISGUISES

The question of *Frankenstein*'s authorship, which the present work sets out to answer, or at a minimum raise doubts in the minds of those who have considered the case closed in favor of Mary Shelley, is not a new question. As has been pointed out throughout this work, from the moment of *Frankenstein*'s anonymous publication in 1818 there have been more than a few reviewers who recognized the hand of Percy Bysshe Shelley behind it. One reviewer suggested that the more discriminating reader would recognize that the author was *not* a first-time author, i.e. Mary Shelley:

> The novel of 'Frankenstein; or, the Modern Prometheus' is undoubtedly, as a mere story, one of the most original and complete productions of the day. We debate with ourselves in wonder, as we read it, what could have been the series of thoughts— what could have been the peculiar experiences that awakened them—which conduced, in the author's mind, to the astonishing combinations of motives and incidents, and the startling catastrophe, which compose this tale. There are, perhaps, some points of subordinate importance, which prove that it is the author's first attempt. **But in this judgment, which requires a very nice discrimination, we may be mistaken;**[2] [emphasis added]

Showing more insight than many of today's scholars, the author of the above review pays particular attention to the thoughts, experiences, and motives in the author's mind, as if to alert the discriminating reader that the key to unlocking the anonymity behind *Frankenstein* lies in knowing the author's background. The reviewer then gives a critically insightful and important hint that although the novel is rumored to have been written by a first-time author, the clues within the text suggest that it is not the author's "first attempt." Therefore, to know the author of *Frankenstein* is to know the mind, motives, incidents, and experiences of the author, *and* the reader must exercise discrimination when searching for the true author. An odd choice of words, *to discriminate,* as if there is evidence that only a select few might be privileged to arrive at the answer—a phrase reminiscent of the Gnostic sects and the secret brotherhoods whose purpose was to pass information along to only the elect, those who were gifted with discrimination. Evidently the reviewer knew more than he was willing to fully disclose but also was cleverly leaving clues behind for the *sunetoi* or *cognoscenti*—i.e., the wise, or those *"in the know."*

The review was not published until 1832 although it was written in 1817. It appeared in *The Athenaeum Journal of Literature, Science, and the Fine Arts* and was written by none other than Percy Bysshe Shelley. It is not surprising that Shelley would have felt compelled to leave a hint for the elect, his own Gnostics, while at the same time writing anonymously to the larger world; it was after all his stated purpose:

> ...I give out therefore that I will publish no more; every one here, but *the select few* who enter into its schemes believed my assertion.[3]

Anonymity, for Shelley, was a way of life as well as a hidden agenda. The desire to go unnoticed was not merely the ploy of a shy young man; rather, it was a pattern established in childhood. From his first years at Field Place, the child Shelley went to great lengths to conceal his identity for the greater effect and advantage he could produce in his anonymity. James Bieri, a retired professor of psychology at the University of Texas–Austin, in his eight-hundred-page biography of Shelley writes,

> His boyhood attraction to role-playing and disguise was another expression of Shelley's ample fantasy life. One incident related by his sister involved Bysshe as a visiting farmer-physician to his only recorded girlfriend, a year older than he, appropriately named Elizabeth, the daughter of the local curate, Reverend George Marshall:
>
> As we were sitting in the little breakfast room our eyes were attracted by a countryman passing the window with a truss of hay on a prong over his shoulders; the intruder was wondered at and called after, when it was discovered that Bysshe had put himself in costume to take some hay to a young lady at Horsham, who was advised to use hay-tea for chilblains. When visitors were announced during his visit to the vicar's daughter, he concealed himself under the table but the concealment did not probably last long. [4]

Descriptions of Shelley dressing up as "a fiend" and inventing characters such as the old alchemist, or the "famous DRAGO, or serpent," and a "horrible decapitated spectre"[5] show far more than a runaway childhood imagination; they form the basis from which a character analysis or psychology of the more mature Shelley must begin. The amount of evidence is clear and substantial that Percy Bysshe Shelley from his earliest years followed a profound commitment to veil his identity and further his pursuits to their appointed ends, regardless of pain or punishment that occasionally caught up with him.

The reader ought to be reminded once more that the argument in favor of Percy Bysshe Shelley's authorship is not intended to rest upon a single proof *in itself* but rather it is in the chain of evidence linked together that inevitably leads the reader back to Shelley as the author of *Frankenstein*. The most complex crimes require more than a single piece of evidence to solve; it is the meticulous search for many pieces of evidence which, once assembled, resolve "reasonable doubt" and allow for a verdict to be made. The fact that this novel was initially written anonymously is one of the most critical and essential links in the chain of evidence—*c'est ce qui a fait pencher la balance;* it is a clincher, perhaps the very fact that tips the scales.

The standard argument for Mary Shelley writing *Frankenstein* anonymously is that it was her first work, it was a horror story written by a young woman, and therefore it might have been dismissed by the public as amateurish and inappropriate. The argument at first glance seems plausible and so it is rarely questioned. However, as link upon link is connected between Percy Shelley and *Frankenstein*, the plausibility of Mary's authorship grows as implausible as her waking dream, while Percy's anonymity is as convincing as if it were his own autograph on the title page.

ANONYMITY: SHELLEY'S SIGNATURE

Shelley's penchant to conceal his identity even as a child became his *modus operandi* as a writer long before the anonymously written 1818 *Frankenstein*. It is essential that the reader observes this point; namely, in writing *Frankenstein* Shelley was following a lifelong established pattern of writing anonymously and as such he was also leaving very clear fingerprints of his true identity upon the book, at least for those "in the know."

Original Poetry

Shelley's first attempt at publishing was a collaborative book titled *Original Poetry by Victor and Cazire.* This book of poems that Shelley wrote with his sister Elizabeth was completed on September 6, 1810, and lived a short shelf life as it was soon discovered that several poems in the book were entirely *un*original and had been plagiarized from Monk Lewis. Shelley wrote the publisher Stockdale and asked him to destroy any remaining copies. What is of far greater importance than the question of the originality or destroyed copies is the fact of Shelley's first publication being written under a pseudonym and the chosen name being *Victor*. Coincidental?

Zastrozzi

Shelley's next publication, *Zastrozzi*, is a short gothic novel in which the main character is engaged in a pursuit, suffers periods of isolation, and is caught in a love triangle that turns toward murderous intentions. *Zastrozzi* was written by Shelley during 1809 but published the year after *Original Poetry*. The title page lists the author as "PBS," another indication of Shelley's design to veil himself to the greater public while also hinting to those "in the know" that he was the author. Bieri observes that there was more to the hint than Shelley's initials in *Zastrozzi*:

> In *Zastrozzi*, Shelley established that his writing would blend his "natural" experience—biographical, unfeigned, and candid—with his more fanciful, imaginative "ideal" experience.[6]

Coincidental?

St. Irvyne

Following quickly on the completion of *Zastrozzi*, Shelley published his next gothic novel, *St. Irvyne, or the Rosicrucian*. This tale, like *Zastrozzi*, borrows on the themes of pursuit, isolation, and murder, but adds the intriguing element of alchemy and natural philosophy united in the hands of an atheist whose end is absolute ruin. Sound familiar? *St. Irvyne* was published in December 1810, and once again the author is veiled while also being hinted at: "*By a Gentleman of the University of Oxford*." Again, Bieri's insight as a Shelley scholar and professor of psychology is worth citing:

> Shelley achieved a strong feeling of the uncanny in *St. Irvyne* by merging the identities of his doubles, two of whom, Ginotti and Wolfstein, have a depth of psychological portrayal not found in *Zastrozzi*. Ginotti, a name borrowed from *Zofloya*, possesses the "'Rosicrucian' ... elixir of eternal life.'" Ginotti's six-page self-description is an early testament of Shelley's need to present himself in his work:

From my earliest youth ... [I had a] *curiosity*, and a desire of unveiling the latent mysteries of nature ... Natural philosophy at last became the peculiar science to which I directed my eager inquiries... I then believed that there existed no God...priestcraft and superstition were all the religion which man ever practiced...now about seventeen...I had dived into the depths of metaphysical speculations...I convinced myself of the non-existence of a First Cause...I had not a friend in the world; — I cared for nothing but *self*.[7]

The very first glimpses of *Frankenstein,* and once again the author conceals his identity and also leaves hints. Coincidental?

The Necessity of Atheism

Following *St. Irvyne, or the Rosicrucian* was the pamphlet which hastened Shelley's expulsion from the University of Oxford, *The Necessity of Atheism* (1811). As has already been discussed in a previous chapter, this was yet another work printed anonymously, though his attempt to cover his tracks was an abysmal failure due in part to the fact that Shelley was seen in Oxford at a local bookstore (Munday and Slatters) placing copies on counters, in the window, and instructing a shopkeeper to sell the pamphlet for sixpence each. When the long arm of the Church of England and the University of Oxford caught up with Shelley he refused to admit or deny his authorship, and for this reason he was expelled. Again, Shelley's literary DNA is evident, but the author refused to attach himself to his own work even if to save his academic and professional future.

Of particular interest is Shelley's calculated plan to advance his tract on atheism to its fullest extent. A new method began to take shape beyond the simple pseudonyms and anonymous writing which preceded *The Necessity of Atheism*. Shelley was growing, learning, advancing in the use of concealment for producing the greater effect. It is worth considering a few details as they relate to this episode. The story behind *The Necessity* is clear evidence of Shelley's adult state of mind, and just how advanced in this plot for his alchemistic and atheistic agenda Shelley had become by the time he matriculated to the University.

UNIVERSITY COLLEGE, THE UNIVERSITY OF OXFORD, WHERE SHELLEY WAS EXPELLED FOR DENYING HIS AUTHORSHIP OF *THE NECESSITY OF ATHEISM*

LETTERS TO ARMAGEDDON HEROES

The origin of writing *The Necessity* took place in early 1811 through a series of letters exchanged at first between Shelley, and later his friend Thomas Jefferson Hogg, with several priests in the Church of England. In his letters, Shelley rarely used his own name, preferring various pseudonyms such as the Reverend John Doe, the Reverend John Roe, Jeremiah Stukeley, and the Reverend Charles Meyton.[8] In these letters Shelley pretended to be a doubting clergyman, wrestling with his faith and seeking some solid advice to refute ideas concerning atheism which he had picked up reading a convincing tract on atheism. One victim in his attack against the "Armageddon-Heroes," as Shelley labeled the leading clergymen of the day, was the Reverend George Stanley Faber, a cleric who was himself a prolific writer, vicar of Rednarshall, alumnus of University College—Shelley's own, and friend to the Hogg family.[9]

Shelley's skill to bait and hook Faber led the clergyman to believe that Shelley's so-called Rev. Charles Meyton was in fact a sincere fifty-year-old conscientious priest who was "unhappily perverted by the pamphlet"[10]—a pamphlet of course also written by Shelley! The correspondence lasted even after Shelley's expulsion from Oxford but came to a swift end when handwriting samples comparing "Rev. Meyton" to Shelley convinced Faber that he had been duped. Prior to Faber's epiphany, though in a moment of temporary suspicion, he specifically asked "Rev. Meyton" if he was also the author of the infamous tract *The Necessity of Atheism*. Shelley, or rather "Rev. Meyton," assured him that he had not written it and had not "the most distant idea" of the author's identity.[11]

Once again Shelley revealed his lifelong attachment to the use of anonymity or pseudonyms designed to bait and hook his unwary targets while likewise denying his hand in the entire process. Notoriety for his name was the least of Shelley's desires; what he was after was to see the effect of his writings undermining the social structures that held humanity captive through tyranny in religion and government. This *modus operandi* is the unmistakable fingerprint of Shelley on *Frankenstein* as well.

Queen Mab

Neither anonymity nor the use of a pseudonym may be, at first sight, applied to *Queen Mab* (1813). Shelley's name appeared as the author and printer, so why include *Queen Mab* in this section? Why would Shelley include his name here in *Queen Mab*, particularly given its revolutionary and atheistic tone, and not in his other works of a similar tone? First, this atheistic poem was not published for the general public nor intended to be seen by anyone except Shelley and a few "select" friends, his fellow revolutionaries *in the know*. The publisher for this private work, Hookham, was concerned enough about its atheistic and revolutionary tone that he left his own name off the printing for fear of prosecution. However, in accordance with English law, Shelley's name appeared as the printer. Two hundred and fifty copies were printed, but only seventy readers were personally chosen by Shelley to receive this work, his chosen few. Even so, *Shelley removed the two pages with his name*, thus oddly enough *Queen Mab* must be counted among those works that Shelley thought better of allowing his name to be seen—perhaps for fear that it could fall into the wrong hands.

Harriet, Percy's first wife, reveals her husband's intent:

> Mr. Shelley continues perfectly well, and his Poem of "Queen Mab" is begun [to be printed], tho [sic] it must not be published under pain of death, because it is too much against every existing establishment. It is to be privately distributed to his friends, and some copies sent over to America. Do you [know] any one that would wish for so dangerous a gift?[12]

In an 1813 letter to his friend Hogg, Shelley wrote that he expected the poem would be "very unpopular" and then added he would be consoled, "like all egotists," if it were appreciated by "*the chosen few* who can think & feel" and by "friends ...blind ... to all defects."[13] *Queen Mab* would not be Shelley's last attempt to write and veil himself, nor would it be his final self-revealing poem privately distributed to those "in the know."

The *Epipsychidion*

Shelley's *Epipsychidion* (1821) represents the high point of his autobiographical and anonymous poems, as well as providing some of the strongest evidence behind Shelley's forethought and intention to communicate messages to his select few. Just as *Queen Mab* was a revolutionary atheistic poem designed to further his agenda among the chosen ones, likewise the *Epipsychidion* contained secret meanings, only in this case the message was far more personal and revolutionary.

Shelley adapted a style of subtleties, innuendos, riddles, and a skillful use of misdirection through fantasy—fairies, flying cars, crystal caves, hermaphrodites, lightning storms, alchemists, and re-animated fiends—all to communicate and further his agenda on various levels; his literary parables to confound the many and instruct the chosen few, his elect.

Although the *Epipsychidion* was published three years after *Frankenstein,* our concern here is not with the chronology of Shelley's work but rather with his deliberate habit of writing anonymously, carefully constructing his words with multiple levels of meanings, and one of the meanings was written for those "in the know" to decipher. In this regard, the *Epipsychidion* is a crucial link in the chain of evidence leading back to Shelley as the author of *Frankenstein.* Shelley chose and applied anonymity with laser-like precision.

When Shelley penned the *Epipsychidion,* he, more than anyone else, understood the autobiographical nature of it and instructed his publisher Ollier to publish it anonymously so that it "should not be considered as my own; indeed in a certain sense, it is a production of a portion of me already dead; and in this sense the advertisement is no fiction."[14] James Bieri notes that Shelley's *Epipsychidion* was

Intended *"for the esoteric few"* …He wanted only one hundred copies printed even though the number "who are capable of judging and feeling rightly with respect to a composition of so abstruse a nature, certainly do not arrive at that number. Further, "it would give me no pleasure that the vulgar should read it. [15]

Shelley, commenting on the poem to his friend John Grisborne, wrote: "If you are anxious, however to hear what I am and have been, it will tell you something thereof. It is an idealized history of my life and feelings."[16]

A clear case in point of what has been maintained throughout this study, *Shelley was at his best an author who could not escape writing autobiographically and anonymously.* The reader would do well to note that although Shelley infused himself into the poems and novels he wrote, he always assumed an audience, though it be small, of those who thought like he did, who understood mysteries as he did, and who would find truth in his hidden meanings.

Once more, writing to Grisborne concerning the *Epipsychidion,* Shelley revealed more of his intent and audience in this anonymous poem:

The Epipsychidion is a mystery—as to real flesh & blood, you know that I do not deal in these articles ...I desire Ollier not to circulate this piece except to the Sunetoi [cognoscenti].[17] [Greek: *Sunetoi*]

Three early drafts of the Preface [Advertisement] to the *Epipsychidion* have been preserved and serve as further evidence of Shelley's multileveled approach as well as his hint to those he expects understand, those few *sunetoi*. In the various Prefaces, Shelley is more self-revealing than in any other writing. In one of the unfinished Prefaces he writes, "The circumstances to which the poem alludes, may easily be understood by those to whom the spirit of the poem is intelligible."[18] In another one of the three unfinished Prefaces he alters the words but not the meaning:

The present poem, like the vita Nova of Dante, is sufficiently intelligible to a certain class of readers without a matter of fact history of the circumstances to which it relate, & to a certain other class, it must & ought ever to remain incomprehensible.

A few lines from *Fragments connected with Epipsychidion* will serve as examples of Shelley writing on multiple levels and using riddles and fantasy to veil his meaning:

Start not—the thing you are is unbetrayed,
If you are human, and if but the shade
Of some sublimer spirit ...

If any should be curious to discover
Whether to you I am a friend or lover,
Let them read Shakespeare's sonnets,
Taking thence
A whetstone for their dull intelligence

I'll pawn my hopes of heaven
You know what they are worth—

That the presumptuous pedagogues of Earth,
If they could tell the riddle offered here
Would scorn to be, or being to appear

What now they seem and are—but let them chide,
They have few pleasures in the world beside;
Perhaps we should be dull were we not chidden
Paradise fruits are sweetest when forbidden.
Folly can season wisdom, Hatred love.[19]

THE SLEEPING HERMAPHRODITE AT THE LOUVRE MUSEUM, PARIS.
PHOTOGRAPH BY THE AUTHOR

And others swear you're a Hermaphrodite;
Like that sweet marble monster of both sexes,
Which looks so sweet and gentle that it vexes
The very soul that the soul is gone
Which lifted from her limbs the veil of stone.

One cannot but feel Shelley's haunting need to tell a personal story, an autobiographical story of the person who does not find a place or partner suitable in this world. A "monster" among mankind for no other reason than the uniqueness which disturbs the sense of normality that the world seeks to maintain. For Shelley, to share his deepest feelings and thoughts, he used riddles, poems, secret phrases and images; he wrote using every literary device in his arsenal to leave the uninitiated reader with more questions than answers. First among his tools was the use of anonymity, to confound the majority and also serve as a signature for the few "in the know." A few more examples:

\|/

FURTHER EXAMPLES OF A HIDDEN AUTHOR

The following list is not exhaustive, but merely serves the purpose of adding additional weight to the evidence already provided for Shelley's use of pseudonyms or writing anonymously.

Address to the People on the Death of the Princess Charlotte

Writing in 1817, Shelley quickly penned *The Address* after the brutal executions of three leaders of the working-class Derbyshire uprising. Princess Charlotte had died in childbirth on November 6, 1817, the day before the executions, and for many people it seemed indecorous to have executions during a period when mourning was called for. Shelley's *Address* spoke out against capital punishment, economic slavery, and the overall lack of respect afforded all women, including the princess who was not mourned for properly. It was signed "The Hermit of Marlow."[20]

Hymn to Intellectual Beauty

In 1817 Shelley contacted publisher Leigh Hunt, sending *Hymn to Intellectual Beauty* for publication in the *Examiner*. Shelley submitted it to Hunt using his nickname, "Elfin Knight."[21] The *Hymn* as with so many of Shelley's works was transcribed in Mary's hand. *Hymn To Intellectual Beauty* was published, not so coincidentally, in 1818, and stands worthy of a careful reading if for no other reason than the date of publication *and* autobiographical references tied to one of his favorite curious themes — communion between the living and the dead:

> While yet a boy I sought for ghosts, and sped
> Through many a listening chamber, cave and ruin,
> And starlight wood, with fearful steps pursuing
> Hopes of high talk with the departed dead. (Lines 49–52)

A Discourse on the Manners of the Ancient Greeks Relative to the Subject of Love & Plato's Symposium (translated 1818)

Although *The Discourse* was not written anonymously, there is a reason: it was never intended for publication. The uncensored *Discourse* was first printed in 1931 in a limited private edition. Not until 1949 were the *Symposium* and *Discourse* generally available as Shelley wrote them.[22] The *Discourse* was an essay touching upon such highly controversial subjects as the nature of homosexuality and the original androgynous nature of mankind as conveyed by Aristophanes. This was written by Shelley when homosexuality was still a crime punishable by death.

Peter Bell the Third

Published in 1819, Mary copied *Peter Bell the Third* as Shelley composed, one of many such works as has already been noted for its importance as related to the final draft of *Frankenstein* in Mary's hand. According to Mary, Shelley put "much of himself" in *Peter Bell the Third*, again a recurring theme as related to his writing. Shelley's poem satirizes Wordsworth and Coleridge, even going so far as to insinuate Wordsworth as "not just a solemn and unsexual man" but also having "homosexual inclinations, like a male Molly." Shelley's pseudonym for his poem was "Miching Mallecho, Esq." from *Hamlet*. [23]

Athanase

Another 1819 anonymous publication, in *Athanase* the primary character of the work was described by Shelley in autobiographical terms as "a child of Fortune & of Power/Of an ancestral name the orphan child." It has been described by Bieri as a poem of intense isolation, despair and disillusionment, a theme taken up in *Frankenstein*. [24]

The Cenci

In 1819, Shelley wrote to his friend Thomas Love Peacock that *The Cenci* was an "eminently dramatic" tragedy well-known in Italy and "generally known among the English." He emphasized having treated the subject, father-daughter incest, with "peculiar delicacy" ... Knowing the play's chance of success was nil if he were known as its author, Shelley asked Peacock "to preserve complete incognito" and "of course you will not shew [sic] the Mss. to any one." Shelley removed the title page with his name and dedication, wanting to preserve his anonymity while the play was under consideration by the theatre."[25] Though this is not argued as the primary reason or cause why Shelley used anonymity, even perhaps with regard to *Frankenstein*, it is worth consideration that Shelley was aware that his name could well work against his hope for finding a publisher.

Oedipus Tyrannus or Swellfoot the Tyrant

Shelley's most savagely satiric political writing... a frontal assault of the monarchy, published anonymously mid-December 1820.[26] Revolution for the sake of tearing down institutions of tyranny was a dangerous and radical theme, one hinted at in *Frankenstein*'s setting, Ingolstadt, home of the Bavarian Illuminati.

Julian and Maddalo

In 1820, Shelley wrote to his publisher Leigh Hunt that he did not "particularly wish this Poem to be known as mine, but at all events I would not put my name to it—I leave you to judge whether it is best to throw it in the fire, or to publish it. So much for *self—self,* that burr that will stick to one." He said Hunt would recognize "two of the characters" in the poem [i.e., Shelley and Lord Byron] and the maniac "is also in some degree a painting from nature, but with respect to time and place, ideal." Hunt saw through this transparent veil, despite Shelley's effort to obscure the poem by saying it was composed the previous year in Este. Shelley also tipped his hand to Ollier, another of his publishers, about the autobiographical nature of *Julian and Maddalo*, saying it was "drawn from dreadful realities." Additionally, Shelley asked Hunt if he gave the "little poem" to Ollier for publication but *without my name*."[27] Again, evidence of Shelley's lifelong pursuit of writing and remaining the anonymous author, even to those very close to him.

〰

FALSE ADDRESSES AND CHANGING HANDWRITING

Shelley also adopted a few additional means to further his covert plans, including the use of false addresses to misdirect the recipients of his tracts and letters. On one occasion, while in the fury of distributing *The Necessity of Atheism* and letters promoting it, Shelley concluded a letter to a young woman using an androgynous persona *and* then mailed the letter from a respectable Lincoln Inn address to impress and misdirect his target.[28]

He used similar tactics of deception in letter-writing with his own father. The fallout from his expulsion at Oxford created what would become a lifelong alienation between father Sir Timothy Shelley and son. As Timothy was a MP, to have a university-expelled atheist for a son was more than a blemish on the family name. Timothy's reaction was a demand for Percy to reverse his opinions or face life without his father's personal or financial support. In letters often more provocative than healing, generally written as requests for money, Percy wrote to his father but soon discovered that having one accomplice address the envelope and another accomplice write "if not there to be forwarded immediately," was more likely to bait his father to read his claims and requests from start to finish.[29] The letters went unanswered. The method of secrecy combined with a skilled performance to cover himself from immediate recognition is simply the manner in which Percy Shelley conducted his entire life. From earliest childhood to the time of his death, Percy Bysshe Shelley remained committed to anonymity as a veil for his agenda.

THE BAVARIAN ILLUMINATI

As has been proven, with each occasion of life, Percy Bysshe Shelley wrote with the intention to gain effect; concealment was his preferred method, a method he developed in childhood and continued to use with greater skill with each passing year. His sister Helen described the young Shelley's antics as construed by his parents as "falsehood,[30] and indeed the disguises and pseudonyms were exercises in deception. This practice he would further develop, perfect, and infuse into his characters—characters resembling himself. To fully appreciate the intrigue and depth of Shelley's "falsehood" as it relates to the *Frankenstein* story is to take particular notice of the setting for the novel, Ingolstadt. This is where our story *must* begin.

INGOLSTADT, THE ILLUMINATI, AND *FRANKENSTEIN*

Ingolstadt was not a random choice nor is it without significance; in fact it is *the* critical link in the chain of evidence leading back to Shelley. Ingolstadt, the setting and the birthplace of the creature, was the birthplace of one of the most secretive and revolutionary societies that the world has ever witnessed, the Bavarian Illuminati. Adam Weishaupt, founder of the Bavarian Illuminati, established his career as professor of Canon Law at the University of Ingolstadt, and also launched the Illuminati on May 1, 1776 from the same city. The Illuminati and its founder were shortly thereafter driven out of Bavaria when several edicts were issued against secret societies by Karl Theodor, ruler of Bavaria.

Documents relative to the plans, organization, intentions, and rites were discovered and published in a four-volume set by Abbé Augustin Barruel. Barruel's *Memoirs Illustrating the History of Jacobinism* was translated from French into English by the Hon. Robert Clifford in 1797–8. Any doubt as to the Illuminati's hidden agenda was removed by Barruel's work, but it also did a great deal to inspire followers and popularize the movement initiated by Weishaupt.

Connecting the story to the city of Ingolstadt is certainly telling and curious, but one might argue that beyond curiosity it does not necessarily prove a relationship to Shelley's life or ideas. Could it have been merely coincidental that Shelley set *Frankenstein* in Ingolstadt? Is there any proof that Shelley had connections to Illuminati goals or felt the influence of Weishaupt when choosing the setting for the creature's birthplace? *Or* was Ingolstadt just a great mysterious setting for Mary's ghost story and lacking the personal element? This book has argued that the Mary Shelley ghost-story waking dream hypothesis was contrived, a diversion from identifying the actual author Percy Shelley, and if studied carefully continually refers back to its true author, Percy Bysshe Shelley. The relationship of Ingolstadt to Percy Shelley, like every other point of contact with him in *Frankenstein*, provides overwhelming evidence of his authorship. The Illuminati link begins even prior to *Frankenstein,* however.

SHELLEY AND SECRET SOCIETIES BEFORE *FRANKENSTEIN*

An early work of Shelley's, *St. Irvyne, or the Rosicrucian* (1811), provides an important reference point to Shelley's interest in secret societies at a very young age. Rosicrucianism is described as

CHRISTIAN ROSENKREUZ

A philosophical secret society, said to have been founded in late medieval Germany by Christian Rosenkreuz. It holds a doctrine or theology "built on esoteric truths of the ancient past," which, "concealed from the average man, provide insight into nature, the physical universe and the spiritual realm.[31]

At the root of Rosicrucianism was alchemy, but not the more common idea of transmuting base metal to gold; rather, for this secret brotherhood the key of alchemy was the transmutation of man himself. In *The Secret Doctrine of the Rosicrucians*, Magus Incognito, the anonymous author, explains,

> ...the alchemy which attracted the Rosicrucians, and which took up most of their time and attention, was Mental Alchemy, and Spiritual Alchemy—something quite different indeed, though having of course a correspondence to Material Alchemy, according to the Law of Correspondence.[32]

And such was the theme of *St. Irvyne, or the Rosicrucian,* in which Shelley developed the mysterious character Ginotti, one who had mastered the art of mental alchemy, appearing and disappearing, changing forms, and ultimately discovering the Philosopher's Stone, the goal of all alchemists, power over death—the secret of eternal life! Sound familiar?

Although the following passage from *St. Irvyne* is lengthy, it supplies a very crucial literary and thematic link as it weds Shelley's alchemistic and Rosicrucian or secret society passion with his pre-*Frankenstein* fiction, as well as establishing the groundwork for *Frankenstein* and the Illuminati setting of Ingolstadt. The alchemist-Rosicrucian Ginotti explains his background and purpose to his chosen one, Wolfstein:

> From my earliest youth, before it was quenched by complete satiation, curiosity, and a desire of unveiling the latent mysteries of nature, was the passion by which all the other emotions of my mind were intellectually organized. This desire first led me to cultivate, and with success, the various branches of learning which led to the gates of wisdom. I then applied myself to the cultivation of philosophy, and the éclât with which I pursued it, exceeded my most sanguine expectations. Love I cared not for; and wondered why men perversely sought to ally themselves

with weakness. Natural philosophy at last became the peculiar science to which I directed my eager inquiries; thence was I led into a train of labyrinthic meditations. I thought of death—I shuddered when I reflected, and shrank in horror from the idea, selfish and self-interested as I was, of entering a new existence to which I was a stranger. I must either dive into the recesses of futurity, or I must not, I cannot die.—'Will not this nature—will not the matter of which it is composed, exist to all eternity? Ah! I know it will; and, by the exertions of the energies with which nature has gifted me, well I know it shall.' This was my opinion at that time: I then believed that there existed no God... Believing that priestcraft and superstition were all the religion which man ever practised, it could not be supposed that I thought there existed supernatural beings of any kind. I believed nature to be self-sufficient and excelling; I supposed not, therefore, that there could be any thing beyond nature.

I was now about seventeen: I had dived into the depths of metaphysical calculations. With sophistical arguments had I convinced myself of the non-existence of a First Cause, and, by every combined modification of the essences of matter, had I apparently proved that no existences could possibly be, unseen by human vision. ... [at that time] a train of the strangest thought pressed upon my mind. I feared, more than ever, now, to die; and, although I had no right to form hopes or expectations for longer life than is allotted to the rest of mortals, yet did I think it were possible to protract existence. And why, reasoned I with myself, relapsing into melancholy, why am I to suppose that these muscles or fibres are made of stuff more durable than those of other men? I have no right to suppose otherwise than that, at the end of the time allotted by nature, for the existence of the atoms which compose my being, I must, like all other men, perish, perhaps everlastingly.—

...Suddenly, whilst yet the full strain swelled along the empyrean sky, the mist in one place seemed to dispart, and, through it, to roll clouds of deepest crimson. Above them, and seemingly reclining on the viewless air, was a form of most exact and superior symmetry. Rays of brilliancy, surpassing expression, fell from his burning eye, and the emanations from his countenance tinted the transparent clouds below with silver light. The phantasm advanced towards me; ...My neck was grasped firmly, and, turning round in an agony of horror, I beheld a form more hideous than the imagination of man is capable of portraying, whose proportions, gigantic and deformed, were seemingly blackened by the inerasible traces of the thunderbolts of God; yet in its hideous and detestable countenance, though seemingly far different, I thought I could recognise that of the lovely vision: 'Wretch!' it exclaimed, in a voice of exulting thunder; 'saidst thou that thou wouldst not be mine? Ah! thou art mine beyond redemption; and I triumph in the conviction, that no power can ever make thee otherwise. Say, art thou willing to be mine?' Saying this, he dragged me to the brink of the precipice: the contemplation of approaching death frenzied my brain to the highest pitch of horror. 'Yes, yes, I am thine,' I exclaimed. No sooner had I pronounced these words, than the visionary scene vanished, and I awoke. But even when awake, the contemplation of what I had suffered, whilst under the influence of sleep, pressed upon my disordered fancy; my intellect, wild with unconquerable emotions, could fix on no one particular point to exert its energies; they were strained beyond their power of exerting.

Ever, from that day, did a deep-corroding melancholy usurp the throne of my soul. At last during the course of my philosophical inquiries, I ascertained the method by which man might exist for ever, and it was connected with my dream. It would unfold a tale of too much horror to trace, in review, the circumstances as then they occurred; ... how dear a price have I paid for the knowledge![33]

It ought to be immediately evident to even the most casual reader of *Frankenstein* that the characters of Ginotti and Victor Frankenstein bear an uncanny resemblance in their passion to unfold the mysteries of alchemy while also immersed in the study of natural philosophy; both men were obsessed with overcoming the power of death, bestowing life, and usurping the role of God. Equally evident is Shelley's autobiographical relationship to both characters in his own alchemistic and scientific pursuits as a child and later as a student at Syon Academy and Eton. Furthermore, Ginotti's reasoned argument against the need of God bears a striking resemblance to what Shelley would soon write in *The Necessity of Atheism*.

The gigantic monster, its horrific countenance, the awakening realization of conquering death but at a terrible price; all of these parallels form a clear picture of Shelley's conviction that the secrets of alchemy, the advances in the sciences, and the power to give life or conquer death, were carefully concealed and guarded by secret fraternities such as the Rosicrucians. It is therefore not the least bit surprising that Shelley's *Frankenstein* would be staged in Ingolstadt, home of the most secretive and dangerous of all fraternities. It is additionally imperative to note that the first Rosicrucians who appeared in Germany called themselves Illuminees![34] The names were changed but the story reads the same, and why wouldn't it—the author is telling elements of his own life and convictions in a fictionalized form in both *St. Irvyne, or the Rosicrucian* and in *Frankenstein*.

BARRUEL, WEISHAUPT, AND SHELLEY

To further reveal the Ingolstadt and Illuminati connection to Percy Bysshe Shelley far beyond the similarities found in *St. Irvyne* is not difficult. Among the academically focused studies of Shelley there are a few that actually take notice of his obsession with Barruel's four-volume *Memoirs Illustrating The History of Jacobinism*, particularly part three, *The Antisocial Conspiracy*, which was dedicated to Weishaupt's writings concerning the founding and purpose of the Illuminati. Exactly when Shelley first discovered Barruel remains uncertain, though most biographers conclude that it had come into Shelley's hands, possibly through Thomas Jefferson Hogg, in his first term at Oxford.[35]

What is certain is the immediate effect of Barruel on Shelley as observed in a March 1811 letter he wrote to the editor of *The Examiner*, Leigh Hunt. In this revealing letter Shelley enclosed for Hunt's consideration his proposal to form a society of "enlightened unprejudiced members of the community" who would "resist the coalition of the enemies of liberty which at present renders any expression of opinion on matters of policy dangerous to individuals."[36] Even more telling in the link leading Shelley to *Frankenstein* and the Ingolstadt setting is the following section of his letter to Hunt:

> It has been for want of societies of this nature that corruption has attained the height at which we now behold it, nor can any of us bear in mind the very great influence, which some years since was gained by Illuminism, without considering that a society of equal extent might establish rational liberty on a firm basis as that which would have supported the visionary schemes of a completely equalized community.[37]

Shelley had every intention, with or without Hunt, to pursue his own Illuminati goals. Recruiting disciples into his plan was evident even upon his first elopement with Mary Godwin and her stepsister Claire Clairmont in 1814:

> At four in the morning, July 28, 1814, the chaise Shelley ordered was waiting not far from Skinner Street. Watching the lightning and stars he wondered about their plan's success ... it was, Mary later said, "acting a novel, being an incarnate romance." A young married father, not yet twenty-two, deserting his pregnant wife and child, was fleeing both the bailiffs and the parents of the two unmarried sixteen-year-old females accompanying him. They had little money and not much more than the clothes they were wearing. Shelley had his usual traveling library, including his four-volume set of Barruel.[38]

What exactly were Weishaupt's goals which Shelley found so life-altering that he would rarely be without his four-volume set of Barruel and would pattern his life around? Weishaupt writes,

> ...that we may insensibly succeed in new modelling the world... The error lies in the means which the sages have hitherto employed. Those means, therefore, must be changed, in order to reinstate in its rights the empire of truth and wisdom. And this is the grand object of the labours of our Order. [39]

Weishaupt envisions a newly modeled world following after the ancient teachings, but as the means were ineffective among the ancients, Weishaupt designs the Illuminati in a manner that its goals would be more effective toward his planned revolution. Weishaupt writes,

> When the object is an universal Revolution, all the members of these societies, aiming at the same point, and aiding each other, must find means of governing invisibly, and without any appearance of violent measures, not only the higher and more distinguished class of any particular state, but men of all stations, of all nations, and of every religion — insinuate the same spirit every where — in silence, but with the greatest activity possible, direct the scattered inhabitants of the earth toward the same point. [40]

Secrecy, invisibility, organized revolution making the greatest use of enlightened individuals—Weishaupt's plans demand a select company to bring his goal to reality. Weishaupt must create his new man, educate his elect, and always use the highest means of concealment to effect his revolution:

> According to my views, I cannot employ men as they are; I must form them; each class of my Order must be a preparatory school for the next; and all this must necessarily be the work of time. [41]

THE ILLUMINATI AGENDA IN *FRANKENSTEIN*

The implications are both frightening as well as instructive as Weishaupt's Illuminati goals are spelled out in a manner that can hardly be mistaken for anything other than Victor Frankenstein bent over his creature in Ingolstadt, a new godless man for a newly modeled world. In Shelley's hands, *Frankenstein* must be seen as a story combining the mystery of alchemy with the advances in science, joined to an Illuminati agenda. Shelley followed Weishaupt's instruction to maintain secrecy, adopt false names, write revolutionary literature while concealing the actual purpose of his writing from the profane.

> Attend particularly to the art of dissembling and of disguising your actions... these three great precepts are to be found in the summary of the Code: Hold thy tongue — be perfect — disguise thyself. [42]

> The first writing delivered to the Novice, to accustom him to profound secrecy is what may be called the Dictionary of Illuminism. He must begin by learning the language of the Sect, that is to say, the art of communicating with the superiors and other adepts without the possibility of being understood by the prophane [sic]. By means of this language, the Illuminees are to be able to correspond with each other, without running on the risk of being discovered. [43]

Not surprisingly, the Illuminist was to take up a new name and disguise his place of writing in order to veil his identity from the world, which was in the process of being newly modeled, while also engaged in creating or forming new men for the new world.[44] Percy Bysshe Shelley was his own man, not one to be drafted into another's movement, but clearly his role model for effecting his own revolution to overthrow tyrannical governments and the Church was none other than Adam Weishaupt, founder of the Bavarian Illuminati. It has been revealed through this chapter that Shelley's methods of writing anonymously or with a pseudonym as well as disguising his handwriting and place of writing, his goals to change the social structures and thoughts of his world—including religion and politics, his literary agenda to use poetry and fiction to advance his purpose while writing to the illumined ones and hiding his work from the rest, added to his secrecy in executing his plans which were emblazoned into his most famous anonymously written novel, *Frankenstein*.

In conclusion, the question must be asked: what is the likelihood that Mary Shelley would have borrowed so heavily on the influences that underscore the agenda of Percy Shelley and then carried over his method of anonymity to disguise an Illuminati agenda in the writing of *Frankenstein*? And supposing that this is exactly what Mary had done, why would this young woman rewrite a preface and intentionally deny any thought or inspiration associated with Percy unless she was also heavily indebted to the same agenda and methods for stirring revolution? It begs the question of credibility and suggests the far more logical solution for authorship, namely that *Frankenstein* (1818) is the product of Percy Bysshe Shelley, anonymous Illuminist.

1 Richard Holmes, *Shelley: The Pursuit* (E.P. Dutton & Co., Inc., 1975), p. 46 [emphasis added]

2 Ibid., p. 195 [emphasis added]

3 Richard Holmes, *Shelley: The Pursuit* (E.P. Dutton & Co., Inc., 1975), p. 46

4 James Bieri, *Percy Bysshe Shelley: A Biography* (Johns Hopkins University Press, 2008), p. 36

5 Ibid., p. 35

6 Ibid., p. 83

7 Ibid., p. 85

8 Ibid., p. 120

9 Ibid., p. 119

10 Ibid., p. 120

11 Ibid., p. 120

12 Holmes, pp. 200–201

13 Bieri, p. 235

14 Ibid., p. 553

15 Ibid., p. 553

16 Ibid., p. 553

17 Ibid., p. 586 N.B., Greek *Sunetoi* suggests the wise, those in the know. It is a term embedded with the same idea as that found among Gnostic sects and secret fraternal organizations such as the Bavarian Illuminati.

18 Percy Bysshe Shelley, *The Works of Percy Bysshe Shelley*, MobileReference electronic text, pp. 1955–1957

19 Ibid., pp. 1966–1968

20 Bieri, p. 386

21 Ibid., p. 358

22 Ibid., p. 410

23 Ibid., p. 500

24 Ibid., p. 479

25 Ibid., pp. 468–469

26 Ibid., p. 549

27 Ibid., pp. 475–476

28 Ibid., p. 117

29 Ibid., p. 165

30 Ibid., p. 36

31 Lindgren, Carl Edwin, "The Way of the Rose Cross; A Historical Perception, 1614–1620." *Journal of Religion and Psychical Research*, Volume 18, Number 3:141-48. 1995.

32 Magus Incognito, *The Secret Doctrine of the Rosicrucians* (Cornerstone Book Publishers, 2009), p. 3

33 Percy Bysshe Shelley, *St. Irvyne, or The Rosicrucian* (J. Stockdale, 1811), Project Gutenberg ebook: gutenberg.net.au/ebooks06/0606391h.html

34 Abbe Augustin Barruel, *Code of the Illuminati* (T. Burton, 1798), p. 1

35 Holmes, p. 53

36 Bieri, p. 119

37 Holmes, p. 52

38 Bieri, p. 284

39 Barruel, p. 76

40 Ibid., p. 23

41 Ibid., p. 22

42 Ibid., pp. 26–27

43 Ibid., pp. 40–41

44 Ibid., pp. 40–41

CHAPTER 5

THE SENSITIVE SHELLEY AND *FRANKENSTEIN*

We shall become the same, we shall be one [1]
— Percy Bysshe Shelley

We are born into the world and there is something within us which from the instant that we live and move thirsts after its likeness.
— Percy Bysshe Shelley[2]

Sensitivity, passion, love, romance, and Frankenstein would seem at first sight to be a subject hardly worth consideration, particularly in a book setting forward a rather focused and deliberate argument for an alternative author to the classic novel. The story is particularly dull for the reader searching for passion, romance, and true love between Victor Frankenstein and his fiancée/sister-like cousin Elizabeth.

The focus of the relationships touching Victor are familial: father and son; mother and son; sister/cousin and brother, i.e., Victor and Elizabeth; and young Victor and his childhood brother-like friend, Henry Clerval. The relationships are platonic in the modern understanding of "platonic"[3] and largely serve as a supporting background to the relationship between Victor and the creature. If *any* relationship within the story bears a resemblance of higher affection, though clearly nonsexual, it is that between Victor and Henry. Victor is loved by others but does not seem to be able to reciprocate love; he is a man alone and obsessed with chasing after his creation. Much like the central figure in Percy Shelley's poem *The Sensitive Plant*, composed in 1820, Victor is companionless:

SHELLEY, THE SENSITIVE PLANT

A Sensitive Plant in a garden grew,
And the young winds fed it with silver dew,
And it opened its fan-like leaves to the light
And closed them beneath the kisses of night.

And the Spring arose on the garden fair
Like the Spirit of Love felt every where;
And each flower and herb on Earth's dark breast
Rose from the dreams of its wintry rest.

But none ever trembled and panted with bliss
In the garden, the field or the wilderness,
Like a doe in the noontide with love's sweet want
As the companionless Sensitive Plant.[4]

Here again, the reader should not find it surprising that *The Sensitive Plant* is far more than a nature poem, it is another autobiographical poem in the Shelley canon. It is worth quoting at length from Earl Wasserman's scholarly work, *Shelley, A Critical Reading*:

Although a member of the garden, it [the Sensitive Plant] is radically differentiated from all the other flowers, especially by its participating in the world less perfectly than the others and by its finding the garden inadequate to its desires. What obviously distinguishes sensitive plants is that, like man, they seem to participate in two levels of the Great Chain of Being, and occupy an "isthmus of a middle state": belonging to the botanical order, they nevertheless respond sensitively to stimuli and seem to imitate the characteristics of animal life, as their botanical name, *mimosa*, indicates. The traditional botanical and biological classifications were seriously under question in the late eighteenth and early nineteenth centuries, and the sensitive plant was one of the most frequent examples of those ambiguous border-forms sharing both vegetable and animal characteristics. Like man, therefore the Sensitive Plant is a native of the world-garden and yet is alien to it, aspiring to its other order of existence; and thus it symbolically reflects the tension, let us say, between the Narrator of *Alastor*, who seeks only whom the world cannot satisfy and who is drawn beyond it by the visionary complement of himself projected by his own mind. Being hermaphroditic, the Sensitive Plant, unlike all the other flowers, is "companionless" (I.12), unable to complement or fulfill itself in another in the world-garden, where it has no compeer; and in this way it has affinities with all of Shelley's aspiring solitaries. Again, like man, the Sensitive Plant is the special favorite of nature and receives the fullness of its ministry. Yet its status is paradoxical in every way, for although it "Received more than all" the other flowers, it is discontent, desiring more than the garden is capable of giving, even though, lacking bright flowers, rich fruit, and scent, it is unable to return any of the beauty it receives from the others... In a world where everything else is fulfilled in a perfect reciprocity of love and beauty, it is at least half out of place.[5]

THE SENSITIVE PLANT IN *FRANKENSTEIN*

It is not difficult to associate the Sensitive Plant's half out-of-place status with the creature in *Frankenstein*. The creature is caught in an existent state that is neither fully human and yet not entirely non-human at the same time. Yet, to keep the question of authorship at the center, note that Wasserman's astute observation is that Percy Bysshe Shelley's choice characters are patterned after those who are most like his own life experience—those who are half out of place, who have received something unique within their nature and must live solitary lives as a consequence of it. They are those characters and people, like Shelley, who were outside of the "normal" social structure. Shelley is the one who is surrounded by flowers in the garden and yet companionless, searching for his other half, chasing that which can never be found. The associations between Shelley, Victor, the creature, and even Walton are uncanny and autobiographically important, for once again *Frankenstein* reveals far more than a ghost story told during a stormy Geneva summer. Shelley is creating characters with plights resembling his own: companionless, identified by their "otherness," searching, and in desperation to find someone suited to be their proper complement.

The Sensitive Plant also presents another curious autobiographical association linking Shelley with Victor and the creature—the "Lady."

> There is a Power in this sweet place,
> An Eve in this Eden; a ruling grace
> Which to the flowers did they waken or dream
> Was as God is to the starry scheme:
>
> A Lady — the wonder of her kind,
> Whose form was upborne by a lovely mind
> Which dilating, had moulded her mien and motion,
> Like a sea-flower unfolded beneath the Ocean —
>
> Tended the garden from morn to even:
> And the meteors of that sublunar Heaven
> Like the lamps of the air when night walks forth,
> Laughed round her footsteps up from the Earth.
>
> She had no companion of mortal race,
> But her tremulous breath and her flushing face
> Told, whilst the morn kissed the sleep from her eyes
> That her dreams were less slumber than Paradise:[6]

The companionless Lady who graced the garden where the Sensitive Plant grew was subject to the changing seasons and with her death the Sensitive Plant had become a leafless wreck and decayed.

> The garden once fair became cold and foul
> Like the corpse of her who had been its soul
> Which at first was lovely as if in sleep,
> Then slowly changed, till it grew a heap
> To make men tremble who never weep
>
> When the winter had gone and spring came back
> The Sensitive Plant was a leafless wreck;
> But the mandrakes and toadstools and docks and darnels
> Rose like the dead from their ruined charnels.[7]

One should not miss the autobiographical association between Shelley's *Sensitive Plant* and the central character of the novel *Frankenstein,* Victor Frankenstein. The grace and love that nurtured the Sensitive Plant was found in the angelic "Lady" whose presence gave meaning and beauty to the garden in which the Sensitive Plant grew. With the loss of the "Lady," the plant's future is destined to be sadness, loss, and eventual death. In *Frankenstein*, Victor's mother Catherine, though introduced as a key figure in his childhood, hardly appears in the story before she turns her attentions away from him and is lost to an early death shortly before Victor sets off for Ingolstadt. It is a key turning point for Victor when he loses his mother on the occasion of his departure for studies away from home. She is the first domino to fall in a series of losses that begin with his pursuit of education. But what of the link to Shelley himself?

Percy Bysshe Shelley's mother, Elizabeth Pilfold, has been described as holding "the pride of place for influencing his [Shelley's] poetic genius"[8] and yet before young Percy had turned two years old, his mother's attention was to be directed to the care of a new child, Percy's beloved sister, *also* named Elizabeth. It is not difficult to concede that Elizabeth influenced the poetic genius of her son; however, determining whether that influence was positive or negative is quite another matter. Very little is known of the relationship that Percy shared with his mother as few letters survive from Elizabeth describing her son. The tearing away of a maternal image so early in the life of Percy Bysshe Shelley is significant, particularly as it relates to his developing ideas regarding women. Richard Holmes summarizes the complications in the relationship between Percy Shelley and his mother, particularly childhood years and the impact made on that relationship as Shelley was sent off to school as a young boy at Syon House:

> We know nothing directly of his relationship with his mother during his first fifteen years, and Shelley rarely mentioned her in later life. From a few stray remarks in letters from Oxford, and from passing references by his cousin Tom Medwin and his undergraduate friend T.J. Hogg, we can gather that the feelings between mother and son were exceptionally close and warm up to the time that Shelley went to school. After this Shelley seems to have found his mother increasingly distant and unresponsive, and there are indications that he felt deeply rejected.[9]

As noted earlier, the image of Elizabeth Shelley, Percy's mother, given by Richard Holmes in his biography of Shelley, was of a loving mother who virtually disappeared from his life the moment he was sent off to school away from home. The obvious comparison in *Frankenstein* is found in the loss of Victor's mother at the very moment that he is to take his first leave of home to study at the University of Ingolstadt.

> No youth could have passed more happily than mine... When I attained the age of seventeen, my parents resolved that I should become a student at the university of Ingolstadt. I had hitherto attended the schools of Geneva; but my father thought it necessary that I should be made acquainted with other customs than

those of my native country. My departure was therefore fixed at an early date; but, before the day resolved upon could arrive, the first misfortune of my life occurred — an omen, as it were, of my future misery.[10]

The occasion of Victor's misfortune and omen of future misery was the death of his beloved mother. In describing the internal conflict produced by this loss, Victor explains,

I need not describe the feelings of those whose dearest ties are rent by that most irreparable evil, the void that presents itself to the soul, and the despair that is exhibited on the countenance. It is so long before the mind can persuade itself that she, whom we saw every day, and whose very existence appeared a part of our own, can have departed for ever... and why should I describe a sorrow which all have felt and must feel?[11]

The turning point for Victor Frankenstein clearly comes at the point of losing his mother in conjunction with his departure for school. The loss of his mother, the leaving behind of his close friend Henry, the separation that takes place with his sister/cousin Elizabeth, leads Victor to seek in himself—and by creating one in his own image—the fulfillment of his own emptiness and desire for self-completion. How closely the lives of Victor and Percy line up.

In her article "Parent-Child Tensions in *Frankenstein*: The Search for Communion," Laura P. Claridge writes,

Previous commentators have, of course, noted Frankenstein's abuse of his monster; strangely enough, however, they have tended to ignore the precedent within his own family for Victor's later actions, as well as the familial tensions that Walton, Victor's shadow self, implies. Such critical shortsightedness has inevitably resulted in textual analyses that fail to account for the complexity of the novel.[12]

Although Claridge is viewing the novel through the lens of Mary Shelley as the author, it is to be carefully noted that it was not Mary alone who suffered the psychological trauma of losing a maternal influence in life. It could be argued, as Victor himself argues, that the "irreparable evil" is more significant for the one who has known and lost such a figure as opposed to the one who never felt the pain of knowing and then losing such an influence or love. Percy Bysshe Shelley knew the anxiety and loss of a maternal figure in his earliest years and the effect of this broken relationship left a profound impact on him and gave expression to his feelings throughout his writings.

Letters from Shelley have suggested that his inspiration for the "Lady" in *The Sensitive Plant* arose from his relationship to Margaret, Countess of Mount Cashell ("Mrs. Mason"), and Jane Williams; however, one can hardly avoid the psychological implications behind Shelley's words: with the disappearance of the maternal power (the Lady) in the Sensitive Plant's garden, the plant itself could not survive, for it was without one of corresponding nature—the companionless seeking the companion. James Bieri observes,

> Aroused and "companionless," the plant's frustration introduces the substitute satisfaction of a maternal "undefiled Paradise" whose flowers (as an infant's awakening eyes/ Smile on its mother)."
>
> The maternal "Power in this sweet place," the Lady who tends the garden, also having "no companion," is an idealized mother: "If the flowers had been her own infants she/Could never nursed them more tenderly." With the passing of summer, this maternal bliss ends as "she died!"[13]

It is the life of Percy Bysshe Shelley and it is the plight of Victor Frankenstein, the creature, and Robert Walton. Consider the words of the creature pleading with his maker,

> My vices are the children of a forced solitude that I abhor, and my virtues will necessarily arise when I shall receive the sym-

pathy of an equal. I shall feel the affections of a living being and become linked to the chain of existence and events from which I am now excluded.[14]

It is to belong to the chain of existence, to find the appropriate companion of like-nature, to find union and meaning by being joined to someone or something which gives meaning, love, and produces the sense of unity that all men and creatures long for. And again, *The Sensitive Plant*:

> For the Sensitive Plant has no bright flower;
> Radiance and odour are not its dower —
> It loves — even like Love — its deep heart is full —
> It desires what it has not — the beautiful.[15]

HERMAPHRODITES, MONSTERS, AND SHELLEY

The Sensitive Plant, the *mimosa*, being hermaphroditic, adds another unmistakable fact related to its author, Percy Bysshe Shelley, into the weight of considerable evidence for his authorship of *Frankenstein*. The hermaphrodite, some have argued, symbolically has the unfortunate status of existing as a living being and yet lacking a proper social identity—"it" is neither a "he" or a "she"; it is an "it" and as such becomes virtually dehumanized and viewed *as if* a monster.

> In Ancient Greece and Rome up until the Republic, beings possessing both sexes seem to have been pitilessly eliminated as monsters, that is to say, as foreboding signs sent to human beings by the gods to manifest their anger or announce the destruction of the human race.[16]

The choice of the Sensitive Plant associated so perfectly to Percy Bysshe Shelley that he referred to himself as "the sensitive plant" when writing to Claire Clairmont, and he also used the hermaphrodite as a paradoxical monstrous beauty in his deeply personal poem, the *Epipsychidion*:

And others swear you're a Hermaphrodite;
Like that sweet marble monster of both sexes,
Which looks so sweet and gentle that it vexes
The very soul that the soul is gone
Which lifted from her limbs the veil of stone.[17]

That which vexes Victor, the creature, Robert Walton, and Percy Shelley through the solitude of life is the longing to find one of similar nature: to be united or *re*united with the missing half of themselves. And yet, as a sort of "monster," where can such a companion be found? Such questions must be asked, along with why was this idea of union or reunion so important to Shelley? It is a dominating theme from Walton's first letter to the sister he has left behind in his quest, or avoidance of his own need for the truly *Platonic* soul mate he longs for. It is Victor's expressed purpose in telling his own story, as a warning to Walton, of what happens when adventures and exploits take over to cover up the deeper inner longing for a soul mate. Victor makes and chases his own demons while avoiding his hidden need for a soul mate, forever making excuses as to why he chooses to be separated from Elizabeth. It is also the obvious plight of the creature who has none like him and seeks his own soul mate, only to live in frustration that what he knows must exist for him is denied to him.

How then does this theme also relate to the companionless hermaphroditic plant and the author of *Frankenstein*? The answer to that question is found in the sacrificial and solitary pursuit by all to find their corresponding companion; it is the unfulfilled longing of Percy Bysshe Shelley and the impetus behind his poetic aspirations, the motivating principle driving both Victor and the creature to their deaths. It is what drives Robert Walton far from home and from his only family, Margaret Saville. For Shelley, there was no greater philosophic explanation for his pursuit than that which was contained in Plato's *Symposium* (*The Banquet*).

PLATO'S *SYMPOSIUM*, SHELLEY, AND FRANKENSTEIN

So important and inspirational was this work of Plato that Percy Bysshe Shelley began translating Plato, *On the Symposium, or Preface to the Banquet of Plato* in 1818, the same year that *Frankenstein* was first published. Shelley's impulsive obsession to translate Plato's *Symposium* resulted in his completion of the work within two weeks. The reader would do well to consider Shelley's state of mind as he translated Plato with *Frankenstein* only recently finished; Shelley's characteristic autobiographical theme reappears as a commentary on what was fictionalized in his masterful novel *Frankenstein*.

The ultimate question about love and the reason behind human companionship arises during a supposed banquet at the home of Agathon. The insightful response is given by Aristophanes, a response whose message is unmistakably the reason why Shelley was moved to translate Plato without any intention to have it published—in other words, it was translated for his own sake. Consider the speech of Aristophanes:

At the period to which I refer, the form of every human being was round, the back and the sides being circularly joined, and each had four arms and as many legs; two faces fixed upon a round neck, exactly like each other; one head between the two faces; four ears, and two organs of generation; and everything else as from such proportions it is easy to conjecture. Man walked upright as now, in whatever direction he pleased; and when he wished to go fast he made use of all his eight limbs, and proceeded in a rapid motion by rolling circularly round, — like tumblers, who, with their legs in the air, tumble round and round. We account for the production of three sexes by supposing that, at the beginning, the male was produced from the Sun, the female from the Earth; and that sex which participated in both sexes, from the Moon, by reason of the androgynous nature of the Moon. They were round, and their mode of proceeding was round, from the similarity which must needs subsist between them and their parent.

They were strong also, and had aspiring thoughts. They it was who levied war against the Gods; and what Homer writes concerning Ephialtus and Otus, that they sought to ascend heaven and dethrone the Gods, in reality relates to this primitive people. Jupiter and the other Gods debated what was to be done in this emergency. For neither could they prevail on themselves to destroy them, as they had the Giants, with thunder, so that the race should be abolished; for in that case they would be deprived of the honours of the sacrifices which they were in the custom of receiving from them; nor could they permit a continuance of their insolence and impiety. Jupiter, with some difficulty having devised a scheme, at length spoke. 'I think,' said he, 'I have contrived a method by which we may, by rendering the human race more feeble, quell the insolence which they exercise, without proceeding to their utter destruction. I will cut each of them in half; and so they will at once be weaker and more useful on account of their numbers. They shall walk upright on two legs...

Immediately after this division, as each desired to possess the other half of himself, these divided people threw their arms around and embraced each other, seeking to grow together; and from this resolution to do nothing without the other half, they died of hunger and weakness...

From this period, mutual Love has naturally existed in human beings; that reconciler and bond of union of their original nature, which seeks to make two, one, and to heal the divided nature of man. Every one of us is thus the half of what may be properly termed a man, and like a *psetta* cut in two, is the imperfect portion of an entire whole, perpetually necessitated to seek the half belonging to him.[18]

Aristophanes' answer to the question of human love is found in the longing that each person has to find their complementary other half. And yet, what if one is the "third sex" or the hermaphroditic Sensitive Plant, or the creature who is neither human and yet not entirely non-human at the same time? What if one is as Percy Bysshe Shelley himself, a companionless creature longing and searching for that which is most complementary to himself and yet unable to find the perfect other half? In essence, just as Victor pursues the creature and the creature pursues Victor, so with Shelley himself—it is a chasing after oneself that dead-ends in frustration, loss, and death.

And so the poet who searched for himself, for the image of the one who would make him One, to complete the truth which was half finished within himself, at the end finds that the search is in vain. Shelley, perpetually chasing himself, the doppelgänger which is easily recognizable in *Frankenstein*, finds in Plato the philosophy to make sense of his pursuit. The journey after that which cannot be found except in the oneness mankind has with Nature repeatedly appears in Shelley's fiction and poems, as Shelley was first and foremost a man whose writings are also his Gnostic-style autobiography.

ALASTOR AND FRANKENSTEIN

In his introspective poem *Alastor* (1816) Shelley wrote of his agonizing search for himself, a search for truth, companionship, and the alchemy necessary to gain the gift of eternal life, or new life— themes which the reader should now notice as unmistakably Shelleyan—and the story behind *Frankenstein*. And just as *Frankenstein*'s narrator, Robert Walton, the searching Poet in *Alastor* "left his cold fireside and alienated home to seek strange truths in undiscovered lands." For Shelley the wandering poet, answers to the ultimate question in the search for unity, companionship, and truth often require the sacrifice of home, and end in the realization of solitude. Consider the Poet's chase after himself, a female vision of himself, as penned in *Alastor,*

A vision on his sleep
There came, a dream of hopes that never yet
Had flushed his cheek. He dreamed a veiled maid
Sate near him, talking in low solemn tones.
Her voice was like the voice of his own soul

Heard in the calm of thought; its music long,
Like woven sounds of streams and breezes, held
His inmost sense suspended in its web
Of many-coloured woof and shifting hues.
Knowledge and truth and virtue were her theme,
And lofty hopes of divine liberty,
Thoughts the most dear to him, and poesy,
Herself a poet.[19]

Wasserman, in his masterly analysis of Shelley's poetry, notes, "The lady, however, is not to be understood as a spirit distinct from the Visionary, a soul to his flesh, but as the union of all that he yearns for in his intellect, his imagination—and, the Preface adds, in his senses. She is created out of the desires of his total nature."[20] The effect of the vision that the Poet has in meeting himself, even the feminine vision of himself, leads him into a predictable Shelleyan pursuit, driven on by a hidden fiend!

While day-light held
The sky, the Poet kept mute conference
With his still soul. At night the passion came,
Like the fierce fiend of a distempered dream,
And shook him from his rest, and led him forth
Into the darkness. — As an eagle grasped
In folds of the green serpent, feels her breast
Burn with poison, and precipitates
Through night and day, tempest, and calm, and cloud,
Frantic with dizzying anguish, her blind flight
O'er the wide aëry wilderness: thus driven
By the bright shadow of that lovely dream,
Beneath the cold glare of the desolate night,
Through tangled swamps and deep precipitous dells,
Startling with careless step the moon-light snake,
He fled.[21]

It is not difficult to connect the recurring themes of searching for that single perfect companion whose image and nature are most like oneself, the longing and frustration of an unfulfilled pursuit which is driven within but under the symbolic form of a fiend, a demonic force at work without and within the soul of the one searching to fill the missing part, to find the perfect other half.

SHELLEY, *ON LOVE*

Shelley's most clear commentary on love is contained in his essay *On Love*. Coincidentally, or perhaps predictably, Shelley penned this essay in 1818 after his completion of his translation of Plato's *Symposium*. In the essay Shelley first declares his own recognition that he is not like others, i.e. reminiscent of the Sensitive Plant,

> What is Love? — Ask him who lives what is life; ask him who adores what is God. I know not the internal constitution of other men, or even of thine whom I now address. I see that in some external attributes they resemble me, but when misled by that appearance I have thought to appeal to something in common and unburthen my inmost soul to them I have found my language misunderstood like one in a distant and savage land. The more opportunities they have afforded me for experience, the wider has appeared the interval between us, and to a greater distance have the points of sympathy have been withdrawn. With a spirit ill fitted to sustain such proof, trembling and feeble through its tenderness, I have every where sought and have found only repulse and disappointment.[22]

Shelley, much like the *Frankenstein* narrator and adventurer Robert Walton whose sister could not sympathize with his inner need to find answers in a distant and dangerous land; like Victor Frankenstein, the alchemist turned scientist whose solitary life and single obsession was to create in his own image that which he found lacking in himself; like the creature whose vengeance is nothing more than a violent reaction to a solitary life lacking the ideal other half, identifies himself to the reader of his essay *On Love* as a solitary man hardly able to associate himself with other men and their affections. Shelley is the Sensitive Plant seeking, longing after, pursuing that Platonic ideal of his missing half, nakedly exposing his deepest need to share with his readers his pursuit after himself.

> Thou demandest what is Love. It is that powerful attraction towards all that we conceive or fear or hope beyond ourselves when we find within our own thoughts the chasm of an insufficient void and seek to awaken in all things that are a community with what we experience within ourselves. If we reason we would be understood; if we imagine we would that the airy children of our brain were born anew within another's, if we feel, we would that another's nerves should vibrate to our own, that the beams of their eyes should kindle at once and mix and melt into our own, that lips of motionless ice should not reply to lips quivering and burning with the heart's best blood. This is love... We are born into the world and there is something within us which from the instant that we live and move thirsts after its likeness... we dimly see within our intellectual nature a miniature as it were of our entire self, yet deprived of all that we condemn or despise, the ideal prototype of every thing excellent or lovely that we are capable of conceiving as belonging to the nature of man... a soul within our soul that describes a circle around its proper Paradise which pain and sorrow or evil dare not overleap. [23]

In his essay *On Love*, Percy Bysshe Shelley has given the most clear and concise explanation for why *Frankenstein* lacks a romantic element: it is a fictionalized account of his own inner pursuit for love. It is the story of two men and a creature, all searching for inner completion and who must put their lives at risk; each man a solitary figure alone in the world searching for a part of themselves which is distant, misunderstood by others, and clearly lacking the expected love affair between men and women which is noticeable in each of Mary Shelley's works *other than* in *Frankenstein*. Could

Frankenstein really be Mary's waking dream without owing even a thought to Percy, and yet be thematically so perfectly aligned not only to his writings but also to the very inner desires of his soul? It stretches the imagination beyond this writer's ability to read the anonymously written 1818 *Frankenstein* and see anything other than another well-orchestrated Percy Bysshe Shelley ploy to hide himself as the author, publish anonymously, and later direct attention to Mary—all of which was conspired with the loving cooperation of his then-mistress Mary Wollstonecraft Godwin.

1 Percy Bysshe Shelley, "Epipsychidion," *Shelley's Poetry and Prose*, Donald H. Reiman and Neil Fraistat, eds. (W.W. Norton & Co., 2002), p. 406

2 Percy Bysshe Shelley, "On Love," *Shelley's Poetry and Prose*, Donald H. Reiman and Neil Fraistat, eds. (W.W. Norton & Co., 2002), p. 504

3 Shelley's idea of Platonic relationships and modern ideas are quite different and the term as applied to how Shelley approached relationships must be distinguished from the modern understanding of a Platonic relationship. Cf. Plato's *Symposium, or The Banquet* with particular focus on the answer of Aristophanes regarding the origin of love for Shelley's understanding.

4 Percy Bysshe Shelley, "The Sensitive Plant," *Shelley's Poetry and Prose*, Donald H. Reiman and Neil Fraistat, eds. (W.W. Norton & Co., 2002), p. 287

5 Earl L. Wasserman, *Shelley: A Critical Reading* (Johns Hopkins University Press, 1971), pp. 157–158

6 Percy Bysshe Shelley, "The Sensitive Plant," *Shelley's Poetry and Prose*, Donald H. Reiman and Neil Fraistat, eds. (W.W. Norton & Co., 2002), p. 290

7 Ibid., pp. 292, 295

8 James Bieri, *Percy Bysshe Shelley: A Biography* (Johns Hopkins University Press, 2008), p. 19

9 Richard Holmes, *Shelley: The Pursuit* (E.P. Dutton & Co., Inc., 1975), p. 11

10 Mary Shelley, *Frankenstein, or the Modern Prometheus*, J. Paul Hunter, ed., *The Original 1818 Text Norton Critical Edition* (W.W. Norton and Co., 1996), pp. 24–25

11 Ibid., p. 25

12 Laura P. Claridge, *Studies in the Novel,* 17:1 (Spring 1985).

13 James Bieri, *Percy Bysshe Shelley: A Biography* (Johns Hopkins University Press, 2008), p. 520

14 Mary Shelley, *The Original Frankenstein*, ed. Charles Robinson (Vintage Books, 2008), p. 172

15 Percy Bysshe Shelley, "The Sensitive Plant," *Shelley's Poetry and Prose*, Donald H. Reiman and Neil Fraistat, eds. (W.W. Norton & Co., 2002), p. 289

16 Luc Brisson, *Sexual Ambivalence* (University of California Press, 2002), p. 2

17 Percy Bysshe Shelley, *The Works of Percy Bysshe Shelley*, MobileReference electronic text, pp. 1955–1957

18 Plato, *The Banquet*, Translated by Percy Bysshe Shelley (1818) (Pagan Press, 2001), pp. 47–49

19 Percy Bysshe Shelley, "Alastor," *Shelley's Poetry and Prose*, Donald H. Reiman and Neil Fraistat, eds. (W.W. Norton & Co., 2002), pp. 77–78

20 Earl L. Wasserman, *Shelley: A Critical Reading* (Johns Hopkins University Press, 1971), p. 23

21 Ibid., p. 79

22 Percy Bysshe Shelley, "On Love," *Shelley's Poetry and Prose*, Donald H. Reiman and Neil Fraistat, eds. (W.W. Norton & Co., 2002), p. 503

23 Ibid., pp. 503–504

CONCLUSION

A Restatement of the Facts

I t is well understood that the final word concerning the authorship of *Frankenstein* has not yet been written. In one regard, this is simply among the first *modern* words to challenge the subject of the true author behind *Frankenstein*. As proven earlier, the first readers and critics of *Frankenstein*, including none less than Sir Walter Scott, challenged the idea that this was a novel penned by Mary Shelley. Like the sea-tossed body of Percy Shelley, time eroded and concealed the finest details which were trademark signs of Percy Bysshe Shelley until all that was left was the Mary Shelley waking-nightmare story which became as famous as the novel itself. In a fashion perhaps most appreciated by a character larger than life, like Percy Shelley, this book has attempted to pull back the Illuminati curtain and test for literary DNA in the once anonymously written *Frankenstein* of 1818.

The evidence presented is not exhaustive but merely a starting point of comparison between the life experiences, education, methods, writings, and social/political agenda linking Percy Bysshe Shelley to the novel *Frankenstein*. It has been shown that the introductory Prefaces differ widely between 1818 and 1831, a fact that suggests duplicity or conspiracy; the possibility that the same author could so easily mistake historic events in the writing of the novel, or worse yet dismiss the contribution of a key person associated with the book, is beyond credibility to any reasonable person. If, as history now records, Mary Shelley was the author, it is an outright lie that she did not owe a single suggestion to her husband Percy Bysshe Shelley in the writing of the book. The internal inconsistencies are proof enough: Mary's supposed overhearing of a conversation about Erasmus Darwin and German physiological writers contradicts her own statement concerning Percy's lack of suggestion toward the novel. Furthermore, it strains the imagination to believe that Mary had forgotten in less than fifteen years that her husband had (at the minimum) edited the book and had made no fewer than 4,000–5,000 changes, according to Charles Robinson's handwriting analysis of the *Frankenstein* notebooks. *If* Mary Shelley had written the first edition of *Frankenstein*, one would be obligated to fault her with the worst form of betrayal by excluding Percy Bysshe Shelley's contribution to *Frankenstein*. Thus the question must be raised: how is it that Percy Shelley has been so quickly dismissed while so deeply involved in the writing of *Frankenstein*? Either the integrity of Mary Shelley must be tarred with the darkest of deceitful brushes, or an explanation must be supplied for her apparent desire to erase all memory of her husband from the history of her first novel. This book, rather than impugn the character of Mary Shelley, celebrates her as a co-conspirator in the anonymously written first edition of *Frankenstein* which was in fact authored by Percy Bysshe Shelley.

But what of the *Frankenstein Notebooks* with Mary's recognizable pen strokes throughout? What of the approximately 70,000 words that were written in her hand? The burden of evidence on this point alone has seemingly closed the case against Percy Bysshe Shelley... and yet, as Donald H. Reiman and Neil Fraistat observe in the Norton Critical Edition of *Shelley's Poetry and Prose*,

> Mary Shelley transcribed for the press most or all of Acts I–III [*Prometheus Unbound*] between September 5 and 12, 1819, and all of Act IV in mid-December 1819. As was his [Percy Bysshe Shelley's] usual practice, Shelley appears to have corrected the press transcripts, making a series of small final revisions to prepare the poem.[1]

The method by which Percy Bysshe Shelley wrote **most** of his poems and prose was by means of an amanuensis. Shelley's nearly illegible handwriting required the use of a near companion, most often his wife Mary Shelley, to prepare his writing for publication as well as to write down his poems or stories as he dictated. His "*usual practice*" was to make final corrections to his work but not necessarily to be the one in whose hand his works were initially or finally written. Thus, the handwriting analysis determination of authorship fails to be convincing evidence that Mary Shelley was the author of *Frankenstein* but rather suggests that the scholars have only identified who held the pen, not who the author was. It is a simple mistake to make, but the consequences of placing all of the authorship eggs in this handwriting basket is problematic and misleading, to say the least.

Another interesting and often overlooked fact that was raised in this study concerned Percy Bysshe Shelley's penchant for writing under pseudonyms or, preferably, in an anonymous fashion. Few readers of *Frankenstein* today would be aware that the first edition of the book was published anonymously, as even the first editions on today's bookshelves are crowned with the author's name, Mary Shelley; this is clearly *not* how the book first appeared in 1818. The fact that *Frankenstein* was published anonymously is less mysterious in light of the fact that it was a virtual signature of Percy Bysshe Shelley to write and publish without his name appearing in the book. His agenda was neither fame nor fortune, but rather to be a revolutionary, and to accomplish his agenda he used anonymous poems, essays, letters in bottles, letters attached to kites, and fictional stories to spread his dangerous ideas. When critics pointed the finger to Shelley after *Frankenstein* was published, it is not surprising that he dodged the recognition and passed the story off as a juvenile attempt by a young woman who was doing nothing more harmful than writing a mere ghost story.

The revolutionary tone of *Frankenstein* was also considered from several perspectives, including Shelley's atheism. The obvious removal of a divine Creator, who was replaced by an alchemist-scientist using the laws of Nature to give life, stands in direct opposition to all that the Christian faith advocates. The story behind *Frankenstein* is more suggestive of a changing world where modern science and ancient alchemy were suitable, perhaps far better, authorities to rely on in the eighteenth and early nineteenth centuries. Few writers of that period were more acquainted with the study of alchemy and modern science than Percy Bysshe Shelley, a man trained by some of the best scholars of the day, including Dr. James Lind. The subtle undermining of confidence in the Church reached climactic force as an innocent woman, Justine, confesses to a crime which she did not commit, simply for the sake of obtaining the promise of heaven from an obstinate priest demanding a confession from her. Who better than an atheistic Shelley could remove the necessity of God the Creator from mankind and replace God with science, while at the same moment lay explosives at the doorstep of St. Peter's Church? This revolutionary idea found its way into what was perceived as a mere ghost story and it fit the pattern of Shelley's revolution, which was nothing less than to tear down the Christian faith.

Another of Shelley's characteristic revolutionary ideas was his intellectual association to the Bavarian Illuminati platform as advocated by Adam Weishaupt. An avid follower of Weishaupt, Shelley was known to travel with copies of his Illuminati doctrine and to share them with his closest friends. The chosen city for the birth of the new creature was none other than Ingolstadt, the university city where Weishaupt taught and where the Bavarian Illuminati was birthed. A new man of science and alchemy for a new world order, so was Shelley's message hidden carefully in *Frankenstein*. Although science was ready for the new man, and the philosophy for the new world was bursting at the seams, it was clear to Shelley that the world was not ready for such a man. Like the Ingolstadt creature and the scientist who fashioned him, Percy Bysshe Shelley was front and center on the stage of this changing world but found that his ideas were unwanted, just as he was unwanted. *Frankenstein* is in some degree Shelley's critique of the superstition of the old world still dominating the leaders and people of the emerging new world.

Finally, it was revealed that Shelley's philosophy of love had much to do with his own sense of being an outcast in the world, searching for his other half—a theme he managed to run throughout the *Frankenstein* story, and a theme he repeated in his poems and early novels. The philosophy for such a perfect, though difficult to find, love was explicitly detailed in Plato's work *The Symposium*, which Shelley was busy translating at the moment that *Frankenstein* was first published. Adding commentary to his fictional autobiography, Shelley completed the circle of writings about love's true nature in his essay *On Love*, written immediately after the completion of his translation of Plato's *Symposium*. Shelley, as the Sensitive Plant, the lone and unbeautiful hermaphroditic plant in the garden, longed for his own companion who would complement him, but found that this world had no such person for him—the very plight which drove Walton, Frankenstein, and the creature in Shelley's novel.

It has been repeatedly suggested that *Frankenstein* is a fictional autobiography by Percy Bysshe Shelley, based on that which he felt and knew most perfectly, his own life and worldview. To read *Frankenstein* as the product of Mary Shelley is to imagine that she, in her short acquaintance with Percy, not only understood his deepest inner thoughts but also had somehow gathered his memories and education and used them to write her own biography of Percy without his notice or objection. To miss the biographical details relating the life of Percy Bysshe Shelley to the primary characters in *Frankenstein* is to read the book with one eye closed and the other eye intentionally avoiding contact with the life and philosophy of Percy Bysshe Shelley.

DOES IT MATTER?

One might ask whether the question of *Frankenstein*'s author makes any difference today. What agenda is behind this book, after all? As previously stated, this book does not seek to malign the name of Mary Shelley in the least; in fact, it offers an explanation for what would otherwise require a complete reassessment of her integrity. Neither does this book seek to toss aside all previous studies and scholarly works on *Frankenstein*; each contribution to this timeless novel sheds further light on the complexity of Shelley's work. So, once again, why does it matter who wrote *Frankenstein*?

What matters most is that the very same issues which gave birth to this novel are presented to us still today: the search for the elusive soul mate; questions about the role of science and healing, regeneration, conception, and particularly the blending of technology and human nature—the Transhumanist movement. Is man a creation of God, or is mankind a mere rat in the scientific laboratory where digital implants, DNA manipulation, and the Philosopher's Stone are still up for grabs by the highest corporate bidders? Is there a middle ground for science to bring all of its gifts to benefit mankind while leaving human nature safely and purely human? Are we on the brink of a new civilization, and will it produce a new race of elites or slaves engineered for the exploitation of elites? Essentially, the questions raised by Percy Bysshe Shelley still matter because as *Frankenstein*'s author, Shelley was a man of science, a man questioning the authority structures of government and the church, the usefulness of peaceful revolutions to reclaim human freedom, and the challenges that face each individual who walks through this life wondering if there is "just that perfect someone," a "soul mate" who would complete all of the unfulfilled longings that every human hopes to overcome with "love."

To relegate *Frankenstein*'s authorship to anyone other than Percy Bysshe Shelley is to miss the underlying human conflict and hope for love in a world where men and women are equally free to believe as they choose, love whomever they find as their "other half," and to be truly free of oppression whether it comes in the form of government or religion. Mary Shelley's iconic name as the author of *Frankenstein* has become the accidental detour away from the issues that drove this novel to be written in the first place, a detour sign well positioned by Percy Bysshe Shelley because he was aware that the world of 1818 was not quite ready to tackle these issues. To answer the question "does it matter?" the answer must be YES! This is the moment to begin addressing Shelley's dilemma, and what better place to begin raising the question than in the schools where *Frankenstein* is still read: by high school students preparing for college; in colleges where students are preparing for their role in the world as the next generation of leaders. As a former college professor and as a high school teacher today, I can confirm that *Frankenstein*, particularly the 1818 edition, presents every opportunity to explore the history of alchemy, the role of science, the social structures of morality and human rights, enlightenment doctrines, justifiable revolutions, the authority of government and various religions, and of course the beauty of English literature in the hands of one of England's finest poets and authors, Percy Bysshe Shelley. Yes, authorship matters.

ENGRAVING BY GEORGE J. STODART, AFTER A MONUMENT BY HENRY WEEKES
(1807–1877)

MONUMENT DEPICTING MARY AND PERCY SHELLEY ON THE OCCASION OF HIS DEATH BY DROWNING. NOTE THE PIETÀ-LIKE SIMILARITIES LINKING MARY SHELLEY'S IMPLIED SAINTLY AND SUFFERING QUALITIES TO THE VIRGIN MARY. ONE MUST WONDER IF PERCY COULD EVER IMAGINE BEING IN SUCH A POSE RESEMBLING THE CHRISTIAN SON OF GOD.

1 Donald H. Reiman and Neil Fraistat, eds., Norton Critical Edition *Shelley's Poetry and Prose* (W.W. Norton & Co., 2002), p. 208

RECOMMENDED RESOURCES

LIFE OF PERCY BYSSHE SHELLEY

Bennett, Betty T., and Stuart Curran. *Shelley: Poet and Legislator of the World.* Baltimore, MD: Johns Hopkins UP, 1996. Print.

Bieri, James. *Percy Bysshe Shelley: A Biography.* Baltimore: Johns Hopkins UP, 2005. Print.

Blunden, Edmund. *Shelley, A Life Story.* New York: Viking, 1947. Print.

Carpenter, Edward, and George Barnefield. *The Psychology of The Poet Shelley.* New York: E.P. Dutton & Co., 1925. Print.

Grabo, Carl Henry. *Shelley's Eccentricities.* Albuquerque: University of New Mexico, 1950. Print.

Hebron, Stephen, and Elizabeth Campbell Denlinger. *Shelley's Ghost: Reshaping the Image of a Literary Family.* Oxford: Bodleian Library, 2010. Print.

Holmes, Richard. *Shelley: The Pursuit.* London: Weidenfeld & Nicolson, 1974. Print.

Shelley, Percy Bysshe, and T. Medwin. *The Shelley Papers: Memoir of Percy Bysshe Shelley and Original Poems and Papers.* London: Whittaker, Treacher, & Co., 1833. Print.

Symonds, John Addington. *Shelley.* London: Macmillan and Co., 1878. Print.

White, Newman Ivey. *Shelley.* Vol. I & II. New York: A.A. Knopf, 1940. Print.

Wroe, Ann. *Being Shelley: The Poet's Search for Himself.* London: Vintage, 2008. Print.

WORKS OF PERCY BYSSHE SHELLEY

*Hunter, J. Paul. *Mary Shelley, Frankenstein: The 1818 Text, Contexts, Nineteenth-century Responses, Criticism.* New York: W.W. Norton, 1995. Print.

Plato, and Percy Bysshe Shelley. *Plato: The Banquet.* Provincetown, MA: Pagan, 2001. Print.

*Shelley, Mary Wollstonecraft, and Kathleen Scherf. *Frankenstein; or, The Modern Prometheus.* Ed. D.L. Macdonald. 1818 Version ed. Peterborough, Ontario: Broadview, 1995. Print.

*Shelley, Mary Wollstonecraft, Percy Bysshe Shelley, and Charles E. Robinson.

Frankenstein, Or, The Modern Prometheus: The Original Two-Volume Novel of 1816–1817 from the Bodleian Library Manuscripts. New York: Vintage, 2009. Print.

Shelley, Percy Bysshe, Donald H. Reiman, Sharon B. Powers, and Neil Fraistat. *Shelley's Poetry and Prose.* New York: W.W. Norton, 2002. Print.

Shelley, Percy Bysshe. *The Poetical Works.* Halifax: Milner and Sowerby, 1866. Print.

* N.B. — The 1818 Edition of Frankenstein was not published with Mary Shelley as the author. The 1818 First Edition was published anonymously. It is the author's argument that the true author was Percy Bysshe Shelley. It is regrettable that the reprinted editions of the 1818 Frankenstein are not published as originally published—anonymously.

CRITICAL STUDIES RELATED TO PERCY BYSSHE SHELLEY

Bonca, Teddi Chichester. *Shelley's Mirrors of Love: Narcissism, Sacrifice, and Sorority.* Albany, NY: State University of New York, 1999. Print.

de Hart, Scott Douglas and Joseph Patrick Farrell. *Transhumanism: A Grimoire of Alchemical Agendas.* Port Townsend, WA: Feral House, 2012. Print.

Goslee, Nancy Moore. *Shelley's Visual Imagination.* Cambridge: Cambridge UP, 2011. Print.

Grabo, Carl Henry. *Prometheus Unbound: An Interpretation.* Chapel Hill: University of North Carolina, 1935. Print.

Grabo, Carl Henry. *A Newton Among Poets: Shelley's Use of Science in Prometheus Unbound.* Chapel Hill: University of North Carolina, 1930. Print.

Grabo, Carl Henry. *The Meaning of the Witch of Atlas.* Chapel Hill: University of North Carolina, 1935. Print.

King, Christa Knellwolf, and Jane R. Goodall. *Frankenstein's Science: Experimentation and Discovery in Romantic Culture, 1780–1830.* Aldershot, England: Ashgate, 2008. Print.

Lauritsen, John. *The Man Who Wrote Frankenstein.* Dorchester, MA: Pagan, 2007. Print.

Morton, Timothy. *A Routledge Literary Sourcebook on Mary Shelley's Frankenstein.* London [u.a.: Routledge], 2002. Print.

Morton, Timothy. *The Cambridge Companion to Shelley.* Cambridge, UK: Cambridge UP, 2006. Print.

Ridenour, George M. *Shelley: A Collection of Critical Essays.* Englewood Cliffs, NJ: Prentice-Hall, 1965. Print.

Shelley, Mary Wollstonecraft, and Leonard Wolf. *The Annotated Frankenstein.* New York: C.N. Potter: distributed by Crown Publishers, 1977. Print.

Shelley, Percy Bysshe, and Lawrence John Zillman. *Prometheus Unbound: A Variorum Edition.* Seattle: University of Washington, 1959. Print.

Veeder, William. *Mary Shelley & Frankenstein: The Fate of Androgyny.* Chicago: University of Chicago, 1986. Print.

Wasserman, Earl R. *Shelley: A Critical Reading.* Baltimore: John Hopkins UP, 1971. Print.

Zimmerman, Phyllis. *Shelley's Fiction.* Los Angeles: Darami, 1998. Print.

PREFACE TO THE 1818 EDITION OF *FRANKENSTEIN*
Anonymously penned by Percy Bysshe Shelley

The event on which this fiction is founded has been supposed, by Dr. Darwin, and some of the physiological writers of Germany, as not of impossible occurrence. I shall not be supposed as according the remotest degree of serious faith to such an imagination; yet, in assuming it as the basis of a work of fancy, I have not considered myself as merely weaving a series of supernatural terrors. The event on which the interest of the story depends is exempt from the disadvantages of a mere tale of spectres or enchantment. It was recommended by the novelty of the situations which it develops; and, however impossible as a physical fact, affords a point of view to the imagination for the delineating of human passions more comprehensive and commanding than any which the ordinary relations of existing events can yield.

I have thus endeavoured to preserve the truth of the elementary principles of human nature, while I have not scrupled to innovate upon their combinations. *The Iliad*, the tragic poetry of Greece—Shakespeare, in *The Tempest* and Midsummer Night's Dream—and most especially Milton, in *Paradise Lost*, conform to this rule; and the most humble novelist, who seeks to confer or receive amusement from his labours, may, without presumption, apply to prose fiction a licence, or rather a rule, from the adoption of which so many exquisite combinations of human feeling have resulted in the highest specimens of poetry.

The circumstance on which my story rests was suggested in casual conversation. It was commenced partly as a source of amusement, and partly as an expedient for exercising any untried resources of mind. Other motives were mingled with these as the work proceeded. I am by no means indifferent to the manner in which whatever moral tendencies exist in the sentiments or characters it contains shall affect the reader; yet my chief concern in this respect has been limited to avoiding the enervating effects of the novels of the present day and to the exhibition of the amiableness of domestic affection, and the excellence of universal virtue. The opinions which naturally spring from the character and situation of the hero are by no means to be conceived as existing always in my own conviction; nor is any inference justly to be drawn from the following pages as prejudicing any philosophical doctrine of whatever kind.

It is a subject also of additional interest to the author that this story was begun in the majestic region where the scene is principally laid, and in society which cannot cease to be regretted. I passed the summer of 1816 in the environs of Geneva. The season was cold and rainy, and in the evenings we crowded around a blazing wood fire, and occasionally amused ourselves with some German stories of ghosts, which happened to fall into our hands. These tales excited in us a playful desire of imitation. Two other friends (a tale from the pen of one of whom would be far more acceptable to the public than anything I can ever hope to produce) and myself agreed to write each a story founded on some supernatural occurrence.

The weather, however, suddenly became serene; and my two friends left me on a journey among the Alps, and lost, in the magnificent scenes which they present, all memory of their ghostly visions. The following tale is the only one which has been completed.

PREFACE TO THE 1831 EDITION OF *FRANKENSTEIN*
Penned by Mary Shelley

The Publishers of the Standard Novels, in selecting "Franken-stein" for one of their series, expressed a wish that I should fur-nish them with some account of the origin of the story. I am the more willing to comply, because I shall thus give a general an-swer to the question, so frequently asked me—"How I, then a young girl, came to think of, and to dilate upon, so very hideous an idea?" It is true that I am very averse to bringing myself forward in print; but as my account will only appear as an appendage to a former production, and as it will be confined to such topics as have connection with my authorship alone, I can scarcely accuse myself of a personal intrusion.

It is not singular that, as the daughter of two persons of distin-guished literary celebrity, I should very early in life have thought of writing. As a child I scribbled; and my favourite pastime, during the hours given me for recreation, was to "write stories." Still I had a dear-er pleasure than this, which was the formation of castles in the air—the indulging in waking dreams—the following up trains of thought, which had for their subject the formation of a succession of imagi-nary incidents. My dreams were at once more fantastic and agreeable than my writings. In the latter I was a close imitator—rather doing as others had done, than putting down the suggestions of my own mind. What I wrote was intended at least for one other eye—my childhood's companion and friend; but my dreams were all my own; I accounted for them to nobody; they were my refuge when annoyed—my dearest pleasure when free. I lived principally in the country as a girl, and passed a considerable time in Scotland. I made occasional visits to the more picturesque parts; but my habitual residence was on the blank and dreary northern shores of the Tay, near Dundee. Blank and drea-ry on retrospection I call them; they were not so to me then. They were the eyry of freedom, and the pleasant region where unheeded I could commune with the creatures of my fancy. I wrote then—but in a most common-place style. It was beneath the trees of the grounds be-longing to our house, or on the bleak sides of the woodless mountains near, that my true compositions, the airy flights of my imagination, were born and fostered. I did not make myself the heroine of my tales. Life appeared to me too common-place an affair as regarded myself. I could not figure to myself that romantic woes or wonderful events would ever be my lot; but I was not confined to my own identity, and I could people the hours with creations far more interesting to me at that age, than my own sensations.

After this my life became busier, and reality stood in place of fiction. My husband, however, was from the first, very anxious that I should prove myself worthy of my parentage, and enrol myself on the page of fame. He was for ever inciting me to obtain literary reputation, which even on my own part I cared for then, though since I have become infinitely indifferent to it. At this time he desired that I should write, not so much with the idea that I could produce any thing worthy of notice, but that he might himself judge how far I possessed the promise of better things hereafter. Still I did nothing. Travelling, and the cares of a family, occupied my time; and study, in the way of reading, or improving my ideas in communication with his far more cultivated mind, was all of literary employment that engaged my attention.

In the summer of 1816, we visited Switzerland, and became the neighbours of Lord Byron. At first we spent our pleasant hours on the lake, or wandering on its shores; and Lord Byron, who was writing the third canto of *Childe Harold*, was the only one among us who put his thoughts upon paper. These, as he brought them successively to us, clothed in all the light and harmony of poetry, seemed to stamp as divine the glories of heaven and earth, whose influences we partook with him.

But it proved a wet, ungenial summer, and incessant rain often confined us for days to the house. Some volumes of ghost stories, translated from the German into French, fell into our hands. There was the History of the Inconstant Lover, who, when he thought to clasp the bride to whom he had pledged his vows, found himself in the arms of the pale ghost of her whom he had deserted. There was the tale of the sinful founder of his race, whose miserable doom it was to bestow the kiss of death on all the younger sons of his fated house, just when they reached the age of promise. His gigantic, shadowy form, clothed like the ghost in *Hamlet*, in complete armour, but with the beaver up, was seen at midnight, by the moon's fitful beams, to advance slowly along the gloomy avenue. The shape was lost beneath the shadow of the castle walls; but soon a gate swung back, a step was heard, the door of the chamber opened, and he advanced to the couch of the blooming youths, cradled in healthy sleep. Eternal sorrow sat upon his face as he bent down and kissed the forehead of the boys, who from that hour withered like flowers snapt upon the stalk. I have not seen these stories since then; but their incidents are as fresh in my mind as if I had read them yesterday.

"We will each write a ghost story," said Lord Byron; and his proposition was acceded to. There were four of us. The noble author began a tale, a fragment of which he printed at the end of his poem of Mazeppa. Shelley, more apt to embody ideas and sentiments in the radiance of brilliant imagery, commenced one founded on the experiences of his early life. Poor Polidori had some terrible idea about a skull-headed lady, who was so punished for peeping through a key-hole—what to see I forget—something very shocking and wrong of course; but when she was reduced to a worse condition than the renowned Tom of Coventry, he did not know what to do with her, and was obliged to despatch her to the tomb of the Capulets, the only place for which she was fitted. The illustrious poets also, annoyed by the platitude of prose, speedily relinquished the uncongenial task.

I busied myself *to think of a story*, —a story to rival those which had excited us to this task. One which would speak to the mysterious fears of our nature, and awaken thrilling horror—one to make the reader dread to look round, to curdle the blood, and quicken the beatings of the heart. If I did not accomplish these things, my ghost story would be unworthy of its name. I thought and pondered—vainly. I felt that blank incapability of invention which is the greatest misery of authorship, when dull Nothing replies to our anxious invocations. *Have you thought of a story?* I was asked each morning, and each morning I was forced to reply with a mortifying negative.

Every thing must have a beginning, to speak in Sanchean phrase; and that beginning must be linked to something that went before. The Hindoos give the world an elephant to support it, but they make the elephant stand upon a tortoise. Invention, it must be humbly admitted, does not consist in creating out of void, but out of chaos; the materials must, in the first place, be afforded: it can give form to dark, shapeless substances, but cannot bring into being the substance itself. In all matters of discovery and invention, even of those that appertain to the imagination, we are continually reminded of the story of Columbus and his egg. Invention consists in the capacity of seizing on the capabilities of a subject, and in the power of moulding and fashioning ideas suggested to it.

Many and long were the conversations between Lord Byron and Shelley, to which I was a devout but nearly silent listener. During one of these, various philosophical doctrines were discussed, and among others the nature of the principle of life, and whether there was any probability of its ever being discovered and communicated. They talked of the experiments of Dr. Darwin, (I speak not of what the Doctor really did, or said that he did, but, as more to my purpose, of what was then spoken of as having been done by him,) who preserved a piece of vermicelli in a glass case, till by some extraordinary means it began to move with voluntary motion. Not thus, after all, would life be given. Perhaps a corpse would be re-animated; galvanism had given token of such things: perhaps the component parts of a creature might be manufactured, brought together, and endued with vital warmth.

Night waned upon this talk, and even the witching hour had gone by, before we retired to rest. When I placed my head on my pillow, I did not sleep, nor could I be said to think. My imagination, unbidden, possessed and guided me, gifting the successive images that arose in my mind with a vividness far beyond the usual bounds of reverie. I saw—with shut eyes, but acute mental vision, —I saw the pale student of unhallowed arts kneeling beside the thing he had put together. I saw the hideous phantasm of a man stretched out, and then, on the working of some powerful engine, show signs of life, and stir with an uneasy, half vital motion. Frightful must it be;

for supremely frightful would be the effect of any human endeavour to mock the stupendous mechanism of the Creator of the world. His success would terrify the artist; he would rush away from his odious handywork, horror-stricken. He would hope that, left to itself, the slight spark of life which he had communicated would fade; that this thing, which had received such imperfect animation, would subside into dead matter; and he might sleep in the belief that the silence of the grave would quench for ever the transient existence of the hideous corpse which he had looked upon as the cradle of life. He sleeps; but he is awakened; he opens his eyes; behold the horrid thing stands at his bedside, opening his curtains, and looking on him with yellow, watery, but speculative eyes.

I opened mine in terror. The idea so possessed my mind, that a thrill of fear ran through me, and I wished to exchange the ghastly image of my fancy for the realities around. I see them still; the very room, the dark *parquet*, the closed shutters, with the moonlight struggling through, and the sense I had that the glassy lake and white high Alps were beyond. I could not so easily get rid of my hideous phantom; still it haunted me. I must try to think of something else. I recurred to my ghost story, my tiresome unlucky ghost story! O! if I could only contrive one which would frighten my reader as I myself had been frightened that night!

Swift as light and as cheering was the idea that broke in upon me. "I have found it! What terrified me will terrify others; and I need only describe the spectre which had haunted my midnight pillow." On the morrow I announced that I had *thought of a story*. I began that day with the words, *It was on a dreary night of November*, making only a transcript of the grim terrors of my waking dream.

At first I thought but of a few pages of a short tale; but Shelley urged me to develope the idea at greater length. I certainly did not owe the suggestion of one incident, nor scarcely of one train of feeling, to my husband, and yet but for his incitement, it would never have taken the form in which it was presented. From this declaration I must except the preface. As far as I can recollect, it was entirely written by him.

And now, once again, I bid my hideous progeny go forth and prosper. I have an affection for it, for it was the offspring of happy days, when death and grief were but words, which found no true echo in my heart. Its several pages speak of many a walk, many a drive, and many a conversation, when I was not alone; and my companion was one who, in this world, I shall never see more. But this is for myself; my readers have nothing to do with these associations.

I will add but one word as to the alterations I have made. They are principally those of style. I have changed no portion of the story, nor introduced any new ideas or circumstances. I have mended the language where it was so bald as to interfere with the interest of the narrative; and these changes occur almost exclusively in the beginning of the first volume. Throughout they are entirely confined to such parts as are mere adjuncts to the story, leaving the core and substance of it untouched.

M.W.S. *London, October* 15, 1831.

GHASTA, OR THE AVENGING DEMON

Original Poetry by Victor and Cazire
Percy Bysshe Shelley (1810)

Hark! the owlet flaps her wing,
In the pathless dell beneath,
Hark! night ravens loudly sing,
Tidings of despair and death. —

Horror covers all the sky,
Clouds of darkness blot the moon,
Prepare! for mortal thou must die,
Prepare to yield thy soul up soon —

Fierce the tempest raves around,
Fierce the volleyed lightnings fly,
Crashing thunder shakes the ground,
Fire and tumult fill the sky. —

Hark! the tolling village bell,
Tells the hour of midnight come,
Now can blast the powers of Hell,
Fiend-like goblins now can roam —

See! his crest all stained with rain,
A warrior hastening speeds his way,
He starts, looks round him, starts again,
And sighs for the approach of day.

See! his frantic steed he reigns,
See! he lifts his hands on high,
Implores a respite to his pains,
From the powers of the sky. —

He seeks an Inn, for faint from toil,
Fatigue had bent his lofty form,
To rest his wearied limbs awhile,
Fatigued with wandering and the storm.

Slow the door is opened wide
With trackless tread a stranger came,
His form Majestic, slow his stride,
He sate, nor spake, — nor told his name —

Terror blanched the warrior's cheek,
Cold sweat from his forehead ran,
In vain his tongue essayed to speak, —
At last the stranger thus began:

'Mortal! thou that saw'st the sprite,
Tell me what I wish to know,
Or come with me before 'tis light,
Where cypress trees and mandrakes grow.

'Fierce the avenging Demon's ire,
Fiercer than the wintry blast,
Fiercer than the lightning's fire,
When the hour of twilight's past' —

The warrior raised his sunken eye,
It met the stranger's sullen scowl,
'Mortal! Mortal! thou must die,'
In burning letters chilled his soul.

Warrior.
Stranger! whoso'er you are,
I feel impelled my tale to tell —
Horrors stranger shalt thou hear,
Horrors drear as those of Hell.

O'er my Castle silence reigned,
Late the night and drear the hour,
When on the terrace I observed,
A fleeting shadowy mist to lower. —

Light the cloud as summer fog,
Which transient shuns the morning beam;
Fleeting as the cloud on bog,
That hangs or on the mountain stream. —

Horror seized my shuddering brain,
Horror dimmed my starting eye,
In vain I tried to speak, — In vain
My limbs essayed the spot to fly —

At last the thin and shadowy form,
With noiseless, trackless footsteps came, —
Its light robe floated on the storm,
Its head was bound with lambent flame.

In chilling voice drear as the breeze
Which sweeps along th'autumnal ground,
Which wanders through the leafless trees,
Or the mandrake's groan which floats around.

'Thou art mine and I am thine,
'Till the sinking of the world,
I am thine and thou art mine,
'Till in ruin death is hurled —

'Strong the power and dire the fate,
Which drags me from the depths of Hell,
Breaks the tomb's eternal gate,
Where fiendish shapes and dead men yell,

'Haply I might ne'er have shrank
From flames that rack the guilty dead,
Haply I might ne'er have sank
On pleasure's flow'ry, thorny bed —

— 'But stay! no more I dare disclose,
Of the tale I wish to tell,
On Earth relentless were my woes,
But fiercer are my pangs in Hell —

'Now I claim thee as my love,
Lay aside all chilling fear,
My affection will I prove,
Where sheeted ghosts and spectres are!

'For thou art mine, and I am thine,
'Till the dreaded judgement day,
I am thine, and thou art mine —
Night is past — I must away.'

Still I gazed, and still the form
Pressed upon my aching sight,
Still I braved the howling storm,
When the ghost dissolved in night. —

Restless, sleepless fled the night,
Sleepless as a sick man's bed,
When he sighs for morning light,
When he turns his aching head, —

Slow and painful passed the day,
Melancholy seized my brain,
Lingering fled the hours away,
Lingering to a wretch in pain. —

At last came night, ah! horrid hour,
Ah! chilling time that wakes the dead,
When demons ride the clouds that lower,
    —The phantom sat upon my bed.

In hollow voice, low as the sound
Which in some charnel makes its moan,
What floats along the burying ground,
The phantom claimed me as her own.

Her chilling finger on my head,
With coldest touch congealed my soul —
Cold as the finger of the dead,
Or damps which round a tombstone roll —

Months are passed in lingering round,
Every night the spectre comes,
With thrilling step it shakes the ground,
With thrilling step it round me roams —

Stranger! I have told to thee,
All the tale I have to tell —
Stranger! canst thou tell to me,
How to 'scape the powers of Hell?' —

Stranger.
Warrior! I can ease thy woes,
Wilt thou, wilt thou, come with me —
Warrior! I can all disclose,
Follow, follow, follow me.

Yet the tempest's duskiest wing,
Its mantle stretches o'er the sky,
Yet the midnight ravens sing,
'Mortal! Mortal! thou must die.'

At last they saw a river clear,
That crossed the heathy path they trod,
The Stranger's look was wild and drear,
The firm Earth shook beneath his nod —

He raised a wand above his head,
He traced a circle on the plain,
In a wild verse he called the dead,
The dead with silent footsteps came.

A burning brilliance on his head,
Flaming filled the stormy air,
In a wild verse he called the dead,
The dead in motley crowd were there. —

'Ghasta! Ghasta! come along,
Bring thy fiendish crowd with thee,
Quickly raise th'avenging Song,
Ghasta! Ghasta! come to me.'

Horrid shapes in mantles gray,
Flit athwart the stormy night,
'Ghasta! Ghasta! come away,
Come away before 'tis light.'

See! the sheeted Ghost they bring,
Yelling dreadful o'er the heath,
Hark! the deadly verse they sing,
Tidings of despair and death!

The yelling Ghost before him stands,
See! she rolls her eyes around,
Now she lifts her bony hands,
Now her footsteps shake the ground.

Stranger.

Phantom of Theresa say,
Why to earth again you came,
Quickly speak, I must away!
Or you must bleach for aye in flame, —

Phantom.

Mighty one I know thee now,
Mightiest power of the sky,
Know thee by thy flaming brow,
Know thee by thy sparkling eye.

That fire is scorching! Oh! I came,
From the caverned depth of Hell,
My fleeting false Rodolph to claim,
Mighty one! I know thee well. —

Stranger.

Ghasta! seize yon wandering sprite,
Drag her to the depth beneath,
Take her swift, before 'tis light,
Take her to the cells of death!

Thou that heardst the trackless dead,
In the mouldering tomb must lie,
Mortal! look upon my head,
Mortal! Mortal! thou must die.

Of glowing flame a cross was there,
Which threw a light around his form,
Whilst his lank and raven hair,
Floated wild upon the storm. —

The warrior upwards turned his eyes,
Gazed upon the cross of fire,

There sat horror and surprise,
There sat God's eternal ire. —

A shivering through the Warrior flew,
Colder than the nightly blast,
Colder than the evening dew,
When the hour of twilight's past. —

Thunder shakes th'expansive sky,
Shakes the bosom of the heath,
'Mortal! Mortal! thou must die' —
The warrior sank convulsed in death.

INDEX